Culturally Responsive and Socially Just Leadership in Diverse Contexts

Ann E. Lopez

Culturally Responsive and Socially Just Leadership in Diverse Contexts

From Theory to Action

palgrave
macmillan

Ann E. Lopez
Ontario Institute for Studies in Education
University of Toronto
Toronto, Ontario, Canada

ISBN 978-1-137-53338-8 ISBN 978-1-137-53339-5 (eBook)
DOI 10.1057/978-1-137-53339-5

Library of Congress Control Number: 2016957868

Printed on acid-free paper

This Palgrave Macmillan imprint is published by Springer Nature
The registered company is Nature America Inc.
The registered company address is: 1 New York Plaza, New York, NY 10004, U.S.A.

Foreword

Let's be honest: we educators often pick up and read leadership books to get new ideas that we can use in our own leadership practices. In doing so, we want these ideas to be wrapped in ready-made answers. This want, this very real need, makes some sense, that is, as educators, we are action-oriented decision-makers. Moreover, the realities of our professional lives tell us every day that the work we do inside schools is hard, and that time, a precious resource, is scarce. But if you are looking for confirmation of what you are already doing in or out of school (or hope to be doing tomorrow or next year) or for ready-made answers, then this book is not right for you. Just stop here and put it down.

Reading Ann Lopez is about imagining possibilities. More specifically, lifelong opportunities that are absent in too many of our public schools around the world. In this sense, Professor Lopez is following a critical and cultural research tradition first beginning in leadership by William Foster, in curriculum by Geneva Gay and Christine Sleeter, in pedagogy by Paolo Freire and Gloria Ladson-Billings, in teacher education by Marilyn Cochran-Smith, and in cultural studies by Henry Giroux, among others. Her work is grounded in culturally responsive practices and social justice, not unlike the recent works by Floyd Beachum and Carlos McCray and other education writers whose aims are, quite literally, to redefine education and in particular the role of school teachers and administrators. But what sets Professor Lopez apart is not only the emancipatory themes found in this book, but also how she shifts the responsibilities for school and social change squarely onto the readers' shoulders, asking us to name and diagnose the problems we face in schools, and then imagine the possibilities one child at a time. This is not a how-to textbook; rather, it is a way forward with specific signposts and roadblocks. Your job is to remove the barriers and design new pathways. From the Preface to the Conclusion, Professor Lopez introduces readers to a family of theories grounded in culturally responsive leadership and social justice. Both families, for her and for me, stand at the center of school leadership practice. As such, she does not review empirical studies supporting the way schools have been and still are. She is not repeating the metanarratives and dominant discourses of governments and business. Rather, she is inviting readers, professionally (see Chaps. 1 through 5) and personally (see Chap. 6) to join her on a career-expanding journey as she explains why schools should make a difference personally, politically, and educationally. Her two tacit assumptions are that her readers are already (1) good people, and (2) good (as in competent and moral) teachers, teacher leaders, or school administrators. In truth, meeting these two qualitative assumptions is hard work, but what she and other critical educators are asking/demanding is that we re-connect schools to communities and to society as a whole so that diversity and equity are not just school reforms, but also social reforms. This is harder work. Having engaged in such work myself, I know that this *ask* is not always well received by educators, who say, "How can I possibly fit one more thing into my already crazy busy day?" I hear this every time I ask for doing more. And yet, as I see it, the obligation of being a public school educator in today's world is to educate ourselves about the real problems in communities and society, from housing, poverty, and violence to underpaid jobs and the future of the next generation. It is our responsibility to explicitly define success especially for those who may not have everyday examples of success in their own lives.

This tradition of community problem-solving goes back to the twentieth century and John Dewey who lived and worked through two world wars, a depression, and a cold war. If you have never read a single word Dewey wrote, please know this: his faith resides in educators and education, a faith strong enough to defeat external enemies whose intent is to end freedom and democracy. Yes, he became frustrated with the many failed school reforms throughout the twentieth century, but he never lost faith in the power of teaching and learning. So whatever you have heard about John Dewey, I want you to know that his ideas on learning from experiences, self-reflective practices, diversity, and equal opportunity for all students were his weapons of choice in solving social and political problems. For him, all children bring human capital into schools, regardless of race or wealth. Dewey said all this when he feared that Nazi Germany might defeat the Allied nations in World War II and take over our schools. Today, there are freedom-loving citizens all over the world who are again living in fear and frustration who are angry. Today's enemies of freedom may not be nation-states; they are ideologies that devalue and dehumanize people, especially women and children. So while numeracy and literacy will always matter, so, too, do character, humanity, and love, including the love of strangers, that is, people who are different from us. Our school curricula, as Professor Lopez states in Chap. 2, involve "the whole environment," experiences beyond the teaching and learning of school subjects. And therefore the thesis of the first chapter is, rightly, dauntless and fearless leadership. Our effort is not just about doing the work well, being competent, but also about becoming culturally responsive and socially just—qualities that are more than a list of best practices in classrooms and schools. That is asking a lot from ourselves and others in education. And for this reason the work gets even harder and more critical.

Educational leaders have both a responsibility and an obligation because we have access to power. Whether we use it or not is a question of courage and risk-taking. Our access to power provides opportunities for us to insert education into political, social, economic, philosophical, and literary discourses and debates. To do this, however, we have to learn how to speak differently both within our profession and also with others from different professions (and cultures). As educators, our audiences are not just our fellow educators or our students, but also the world's citizens (including refugees and so-called illegal aliens), people from all cultures, religions, and ideologies. At one time in recent history, educators were seen as statesmen/women and acted as such. We need to remember and bring that mindset back into school leadership.

Further, we have a moral responsibility to teach teachers, students, and community members about the moral use of power. Here, too, we cannot equate being educated with being schooled. Some observers, including John Dewey, traveled to Germany to study its notable school system only to conclude that high numeracy and literacy levels were no guarantees for creating a great nation/world. Competency is not character. Yes, as humans, we are imperfect; and yes, the outcomes and consequences of our planned actions involve that which is unintended and unpredictable. None of us live and work in a controlled science laboratory. Our work—in and out of schools—is in the real world.

As such, the work is difficult, more so when it comes to culturally responsive leadership and social justice. The *ask* from these two theories-in-action involves our being present and active in students' lives, where they and their families live. The *ask* calls for our bringing together of school and community in new and different ways. The key point is that we have to do this work ourselves, not through state, provincial, or district mandates, but as school leaders. The reality is that we never come to education prepared for this challenge. In Chap. 6, Professor Lopez describes how she felt at first. "As I reflect on my journey I have developed and gained a deeper understanding of what it means to navigate complex school environments. I am supported on this journey by critical friends and my own commitment not to give up even when the journey becomes tough. There were moments when I felt powerless and afraid to act, but I grew stronger in my own sense of agency and commitment. Culturally responsive leadership and social justice leadership is a process that involves continuous learning and unlearning, that raises complex questions about the roles and responsibilities of school leaders. The tension between learning and unlearning, and realigning one's professional identity between old and new, is an important story to tell by educational leaders."

It is in this personal/professional self-reflection that we see the gist of the many contemporary criticisms made against what are called neoliberal policies and market forces. These are terms thrown around by academics, not by practitioners and citizens. But what it means to Professor Lopez is that unless educators take back schooling, its curriculum, and our school leadership from external authorities, our thoughts and actions will be driven by others out of compliance and fear—of losing one's job. We become paradoxically powerless to act as culturally responsive and social justice leaders. We become managerial in the sense of working long hours to maintain the existing school and district cultures by following pathways and practices that are already in place. And in so doing, we lose the right to call our practice leadership. Our daily choices are safe choices, doing what others want us to do; our judgments are put on hold; school improvement becomes student achievement, which becomes raising test scores; learning becomes knowledge transmission not curiosity and inquiry. This is more than the clichéd slippery slope. This is the negation of education, the negation of being human, of making professional judgments and of learning from mistakes. To read Professor Lopez is to open ourselves up to rethinking the meanings and possibilities for school leadership. She reminds us in Chap. 2 that "School leaders are under tremendous pressure to respond to the growing diversity in schools that have become a mirror into the social changes that are taking place in society. Schools have become cultural spaces where dialogue and discourse occurs and represent the contradictions of society where understanding and meanings are teased out at the same time tensions are explored".

Again in Chap. 6 Lopez personalizes these challenges: "I was not fully prepared as a racial minority to traverse the difficult and tension-filled conversations about race that often occur in schools (Cho, 2011). I had not anticipated the feelings of pain and trauma that such moments would evoke. At times I felt angry and anxious and worn down by the racist attitudes toward me from some staff members. Sometimes racial minorities are afraid of expressing how we feel and the impact of racism in schools because we are fearful of being accused of playing the race card and suppress the pain we feel. It is important, however, to examine and theorize and come to an understanding of ways to be empowered and carry on the work".

In conclusion, I ask you to see how Professor Lopez uses the word "theory" as a dynamic theory-in-action. In this sense, we live and breathe theory; we don't gaze at it from afar. Social justice, as the term implies, is quite literally "social" as in our many relationships with others. I know that educators get hung up on definitions—as we do with the terms standards, benchmarks, objectives, and goals. But in today's world, more than ever before, we need to embrace pluralism, diversity, and imaginative possibilities. Thus, social justice is meant to be a deliberate intervention to solve real-world problems, correct accidents and circumstances (e.g., demography/zip codes as destiny), be inclusive of everyone everywhere, disrupt injustices, and most of all be measured by consequences (i.e., material differences), rather than by our good intentions or sincere caring. Social justice is meant to make a material difference in people's everyday lives. And, as such, social justice is a necessary educational idea in the real world.

Questioning and Unpacking versus Answering and Unwrapping

Leadership means many things to each of us: from school improvement to social change; from knowledge transmission to transformative learning and curriculum inquiry, a matter of a life worth living (self-reflection). A moral commitment to others especially those minors in our care—there can be no greater injustice than an adult who does harm to children and adolescents.

So That We Can Rethink Our Own Notions of Leadership

What are we to make of scholars who say that neo-liberal policies and politics are destroying public education? For one thing, the notion of neo-liberal is affixed to certain policies that originate outside of education, but which have been embraced wittingly and unwittingly by educators. Some scholars see bogeymen in competition, entrepreneurship, market forces ... but why have these human and cultural traits/behaviors been demonized by critical and liberal writers? My dispute is with any policy that hinders educators from thinking for themselves and acting both on their experiences in classrooms and life and their professional education... to separate education from thinking trivializes the possibilities and potential of human beings. One need not have grand ideas to simply want to act in accordance with his or her own judgments. And through those judgments keep an open mind to better ideas, better ways of behaving (toward one another).

Ira Bogotch
Florida Atlantic University
Boca Raton, FL, USA

Preface

Education has a moral purpose to make a difference in the lives of students regardless of background (Fullan, 2003, 2014). Many schools are experiencing rapid growth in the number of students of color, culturally and linguistically diverse students, students from low-income families and students with many different identities. However, all is not well as some view the increasing diversity as a problem rather than an opportunity (Banks, 2007; Howard, 2007). Some strides have been made with various initiatives and policies to support diverse students, but more work needs to be done as research continues to show that some students are not faring well in the education system. For the advancement of society it is important that all students are prepared and educated, so that they can contribute meaningfully to society. I believe that education should be a vehicle for social change. It is important for educators to challenge the systems and barriers that stand in the way of success for some students, and posit new and alternative ways of achieving equity for all. This can be done through on-going inquiry at all levels of the education system. Inquiry is a fundamental aspect of any educational endeavor, because it is through inquiry that we look back, see new possibilities ahead, and create change.

This book has been a dream and a vision since my first days as a teacher. I come to this work informed by my experiences in very diverse contexts: as a classroom teacher, school administrator, teacher educator, university professor and administrator, and as a Black woman who believes that the educational system has a responsibility to ensure that all students have the opportunity to succeed. I walk in the footsteps of scholars and educators who have championed the cause of the underserved and underrepresented in the educational system, from kindergarten to higher education. I argue that education should be empowering and socially just. My philosophy of what education should be and can be has been honed by the struggles and histories of the Jamaican people, and my coming of age, so to speak, in the 1980s. A time when our leaders dared to challenge the status quo make education a right for all, and most importantly make post secondary education affordable to those who could not otherwise have paid to attend university. My years at the University of the West Indies, Mona Campus Kingston Jamaica started me on a journey to fight for greater equity in education. The themes of equity, diversity, and social justice are reflected in my teaching, research, and scholarly pursuits.

We live in a world where borders are shrinking, people are on the move, and those who have been marginalized, excluded, and oppressed are insisting on being heard, valued, and included, while some are trying to hold onto the vestiges of the past. Recent federal elections in Canada and the fight for the presidency of the USA bring these contrasts to the forefront of the social discourse. Education is not exempt from this debate. In fact, it is front and center as Western societies in these times of social change wrestle with questions of what the role of education should be. I see my role as a critical educator to be agentive and to act on behalf of students, but most importantly to support students who have been marginalized and who have not well served by the education system. We must take risks, disrupt exclusionary norms and practices, and seek out spaces for critical action Lopez & Olan (Forthcoming). By critical action I mean engaging in practices that challenge the status quo and power. Through critical theoretical frameworks we excavate biases and assumptions that we hold and see what is possible in our sphere of influence. In my own teaching I urge students to engage with issues that are tension-filled and reinforce the notion that learning occurs from and through discomfort.

Culturally responsive and social justice leadership theoretical frameworks ground this work. I also acknowledge other critical frameworks and discourses that have contributed and continue to contribute to my understanding of ways to better serve diverse students, students of color and those who have traditionally been underserved by the education system. Theoretical frameworks such as critical multicultural education (Banks, 2005; Grant & Sleeter, 2011) and antiracist education (Dei, 1995; Lee, 2009) are very relevant to school leaders who work to create change in their schools and communities. Most would argue however, notwithstanding subtle interpretations that these theoretical frameworks advocate for similar educational outcomes for students. My work as a school leader, scholar, teacher, university professor, and researcher is grounded in these critical theoretical frameworks. In this book I seek to amplify and tease out ways that these critical theoretical frameworks, particularly culturally responsive and social justice leadership can be implemented and inform the work of practitioners. – theory to action.

Why another book about culturally responsive and socially just leadership? The answer is the job is not done. Far too many students from communities of color, poor students, and students from ethnically and culturally diverse backgrounds are not succeeding in school. School leaders must continue to work to create schools that reflect and include their experiences, values, and needs. The aim of this book is to add to ways that practitioners can continue their work on behalf of students who have been traditionally underserved, recognizing the inherent tensions, challenges, and complexities. It is my hope that this book will add to the growing body of work that offers practical examples of ways that culturally responsive and socially just leadership can be enacted. Brooks (2012) reminds us that social justice action can be any small act that changes the experience of students. This can be as quiet and calm as a teacher's caring and compassionate look, or as unrelenting as the fury that a bold and courageous teacher or professor unleashes on a racist colleague. Culturally responsive leadership and social justice leadership are about hope and optimism.

While there still remains definitional ambiguity of leadership, in practice it is about the choices that are made in schools, from the classroom to the front office, that impact the educational experiences and lives of students. Leadership involves influence, values, vision and power. As such leadership and those who lead matter. Sergiovanni (1992) suggests that everyone is a leader and that leadership is about doing what is right for all students as the basis of decisions and actions. Sergiovanni argued further that head, heart, and mind must work together in leadership so that new ways of knowing can emerge through risk taking and student-centered learning in a climate where values and attitudes are posited and challenged in dialogic ways. Leaders matter: what they think say and do, who they are, and how they go about the act of leading (Sparks, 2005). Leadership has been advanced as a crucial ingredient in bringing about change in schools and improving learning outcomes for students, second only to teaching (Leithwood, Louis, Anderson, & Wahlstrom, 2004). Fraise and Brooks (2015) argue that leadership is about the agency of educational leaders throughout the school community, that includes formal and informal educators, families, and communities.

Leadership must be about change. Educational leaders must make sense of the changes that are taking place in their contexts given the demographic shifts taking place in society. Leaders are important to the success of the educational system and are relevant in implementing and bringing about change.

The increasing diversity in schools is a phenomena of the twenty-first century and this is not lost on policy makers and educators. How educational leaders make sense of the issues they face define their actions and decisions on school programs, policies, and practices (Evans, 2007). In some respects the changes that have taken place within neo-liberal educational agendas have not been successful in developing a robust understanding of equity, and this calls for more critical approaches to dealing with issues of diversity (Portelli, 2011).

Darling-Hammond (2011) notes that growing diversity in schools poses serious challenges for educators. In public education where social relationships are mediated by race, ethnicity, and constructions of social difference, equity, and inclusion makes particular demands upon the educational agenda (Solomon & Levine-Rasky, 2003). Critical educational leadership scholars (Bogotch, 2002; Jean-Marie, 2008; Jean-Marie & Normore, 2010; Ryan, 2014; Shields, 2010; Theoharis, 2007) have argued that centering social justice and critical approaches at the heart of the educational leadership discourse on diversity will create positve change. They suggest moving beyond theorizing to offering workable and practical solutions that practitioners can implement in their daily work. In other words, bridging the theory—practice gap that is so often written and talked about in education discourse.

Education in any society must build social awareness and articulate a future that is grounded in the material, emotional, and spiritual needs of our lives (Shapiro & Shapiro, 1995). In an era when social justice and equity have become buzzwords, and diversity continues to be seen as something to be embraced, tolerated, or managed, I advocate in this book for critical approaches that challenge dominant ideologies and knowledge. I share practices and reflections that educational leaders might find useful as they traverse their leadership journey. Our purpose as culturally responsive and social justice educators is to seriously examine the role of critical theories as the basis for a high-quality, academically excellent education by examining the social disparities that create inequities (Shields & Mohan, 2008).

The call for more critical approaches in education is not new. From Dewey to Freire, democracy and the plight of the oppressed have been in the educational discourse. Dewey (1938) pointed out that education will inevitably be a site of struggle, practically and theoretically. Freire (1970) argued that the poor and oppressed must be provided with educational experiences that make it possible for them to take control of their lives. Those who embrace a critical stance must critique social injustice, think critically, take risks, be curious, and question existing taken-for-granted practices.

The goal of this book is to elucidate what culturally responsive and socially just leadership practices might look like in diverse contexts. It is based on the experiences and narratives of school leaders (principals, vice principals and teacher leaders), all of whom who worked in schools where they committed to doing culturally responsive and social justice work. Through their narratives they share the successes, tensions, and challenges of being culturally responsive and socially just school leaders. Educational leaders must continue to search for ways of approaching leadership in diverse school contexts, and develop theoretical frameworks of inclusion and equity that translate into meaningful practice. This is not an easy task. To be effective in schools that are becoming increasingly more diverse, educational leaders must move beyond the diversity training that has become popularized, but is nothing more than window dressing that does not address some of the more troubling issues that impact minoritized students. This rhetoric has permeated education and has given rise to a cottage industry of diversity activities with feel-good sound bites without much real change taking place in the lives of students. Educational leaders must develop clear, congruent personal and professional ideologies that support diversity, equity, and inclusiveness (Evans, 2007).

This book is based on research that I conducted with fourteen school leaders in the Greater Toronto Area which focused on how they implemented culturally responsive practices grounded in culturally responsive and social justice theoretical frameworks in their schools, parts of which have been published elsewhere (Lopez, 2015, 2016b). My own experiences as a Black school leader also informs this book. The school leaders in the study described their educational practices as culturally responsive. The school leaders who participated in the study were from diverse demographic backgrounds themselves and worked in very diverse schools, both elementary and secondary. They had varying levels of experience, ranging from five years to over thirty-five years. Participants self-identified as being or belonging to the following groups: African Canadian, Black, South Asian, White, female, male, Muslim, immigrant, and Caribbean (Jamaican, Guyanese, Trinidadian). Eleven of the participants self-identified as female and three as male. Participants were leaders in their schools in various capacities and had various leadership roles-resource teachers, instructional leaders department heads vice principals and principals. Eight participants were school administrators (principals and vice principals) and six were teachers leaders, resource teachers, department heads). Six worked in elementary schools, seven in secondary schools, and one participant worked as a lead in a welcome center that supports newcomers to Canada entering that school board. Study participants were recruited mainly through emails sent to school leaders who I had come to know through various contexts, as well as referrals by other educators. A qualitative research approach methodology was employed (Carspecken, 1996; Denzin & Lincoln, 2005). Data were collected utilizing open-ended questionnaires and semi-structured interviews. The following questions guided the research:

1. How and why do educational leaders embark on a journey of culturally responsive leadership?
2. What practices do culturally responsive leaders engage in and why?
3. What challenges and tensions do culturally responsive leaders face?
4. In what ways might culturally responsive leaders be mentored, supported, and sustained?
5. How would you describe the effectiveness of culturally responsive leadership practices in your school and the impact on student engagement and achievement?

Participants in the study shared practices they deemed culturally responsive and advanced a social justice agenda in their schools, successes they experienced, as well as areas of tension and challenges. I argue that these school leaders are the embodiment of fearless and dauntless leaders, who stand up for equity, diversity, and social justice. They epitomize courageous leadership. I thank my participants for sharing their stories and journeys with me. In many ways I was an insider in this research given my experience as a former classroom teacher, department head, and secondary school administrator in the public school system in Ontario. Because of this I was able to connect to their narratives, struggles and challenges. The insider researcher holds prior knowledge and understandings of the group, brings deeper insights to the research through the reflexive process of data collection and analysis, in order to reach a deeper level of introspection that may assist them in the narration of their participants' stories (Greene, 2014).

This work is about transfomative action and critical inquiry. Critical inquiry is rigorous, and involves collaboratively informed school-based dialectic questions such as what are the educational goals of school programs and instructional practices (Sirotnik, 1998). The essence of critical inquiry is the willingness and ability of people to engage in discourse and dialogue that challenge their beliefs, knowledge, existing norms, and practices. Critical educational practices deal specifically with an understanding of resistance to hierarchies and systems of domination (Dei, James, Karumanchery, James-Wilson, & Zine, 2000). Posner (1998) suggests that critical education examines what counts as legitimate knowledge, ways that schools reproduce and perpetuate hegemonic practices, and what is valued as curriculum. McLaren (1998) argues that critical education is a site of struggle over meaning, power, and relations. Critical educators must engage in an ideology of social justice, and live with the understanding that knowledge is always partial and incomplete, and that critical pedagogy and practices can be an uncomfortable and self-contesting exercise (McLaren, 1995). It is not enough for educators to embrace critical theoretical frameworks; theory must be linked to practices and behaviors (Montano, Lopez-Torres, DeLissovoy, Pacheo, & Stillman, 2002).

This is a book about ways that practicing school leaders and other practitioners can bring theory and practice together, challenge inequities in the educational system, and harness the potential offered by the growing diversity in schools. School leaders who are interested in culturally responsive and social justice education must continue to seek out ways to bring ideas to action, bring theory to practice, and answer questions such as: What does culturally responsive leadership looks like in my school or classroom? How do I start on a journey of culturally responsive leadership? How do I develop a critical and robust understanding of equity and diversity? What beliefs and practices do I need to learn and unlearn on this journey? Where can I find culturally responsive resources? How do I deal with resistance to my work, my beliefs, and sometimes my identity? How do I change my practice to be more culturally responsive and socially just? While one book cannot answer all of these questions, my hope is that practicing school leaders will find it useful as they seek answers to these questions.

This book is also about praxis - that is translating theory into action with the hope of creating positve and meaningful change in the lives of students. Praxis is also about reflection and action. Because our actions affect others, praxis is inherently political (Tierney & Sallee, 2008). When school leaders engage in praxis there must be a commitment to challenging the status quo and advocating for those who have been oppressed and marginalized (Freire, 1970). Freire warned against abstract theorizing without action, and action without deep understanding and reflection. He suggested that educators take action within a theoretical framework of thought and critical inquiry with others, and engage in creative reflection and action in order to change the world. Educational leaders who engage in praxis grounded in critical frameworks seek to create change in the lives of diverse students, students of color, Aboriginal students, students from low socio-economic backgrounds, students with different abilities, students who identify as gay, lesbian, and transgendered, and all those who have been marginalized and excluded from the education process. Schools are diverse contexts and spaces that students occupy and their interests are not always reflected in policies and practices. It is impossible to focus on all aspects of diversity in one book, so much of the focus of this book will be on cultural, ethnic, language, racial, and socio-economic aspects of diversity the aspects of diversity that were more evident in the narratives that participants shared. Gay (2010) notes that it is important for authors and teachers to declare how they understand and engage with diversity, not that one set of priorities are right or wrong but they should make their commitments explicit. We do know however that efforts that address specific aspects of diversity are beneficial overall.

Supporting diverse students' identities is fundamental to creating change in the school system, a task that requires all stakeholders to work together to create educational spaces that engage with difference as an asset and foster open-mindedness in an effort to create socially just learning environments (Singer, 2011). Educators working together to achieve social justice, challenge oppression and inequities in the education system is important work (Lopez, 2005). Educational leaders in diverse schools must move beyond blame and befuddlement and work to transform themselves and their schools to serve all their students well (Howard, 2007).

Organization of the Book

This book is about turning theory into action with the hope that it will be useful for practitioners. At the end of each chapter I include what I call "Think Alouds" or questions for reflection. I sometimes refer to these as "Think Abouts". These are questions that students in educational leadership and principal preparation courses, as well as practicing school leaders can use to guide their thinking about the issues and engage in dialogue. I have used "Think Alouds" and "Think Abouts" in my own teaching for a long time and found them to be useful in engaging students in critical dialogue. I also include research activities at the end of each chapter to encourage users of the book, be they students, practitioners or others, to continue to examine areas that might be of interest and to build their own knowledge and understanding. It is important for leaders to continuously examine the assumptions that they bring to their role. As Sparks (2005) argues, leaders must consider their assumptions, their understanding of the issues, as well as behaviors that might perpetuate current practices.

The book is divided into six chapters and a conclusion. Chapter 1 discusses the current context in schools today in Canada and the USA and indeed most Western countries. Chapter 2 examines the notion of critical education that informs the book, as well as culturally responsive and social justice leadership theories. Chapter 3 makes the connection between culturally responsive leadership and student engagement, based on the experiences of the study participants, and posits a student engagement framework that centers on issues of diversity. Chapter 4 explores the tensions, struggles, and challenges of school leaders who engage in culturally responsive and socially just leadership practices. Chapter 5 looks at the kinds of support and sustenance that might benefit educational leaders on this journey. It draws not only on research with educational leaders, but on research that I conducted previously with teacher leaders and my own doctoral research. I posit the notion of collaborative mentorship as a form of support and sustenance. Chapter 6 encapsulates my own experiences as a Black educational leader, while Chapter 7 offers concluding thoughts and focuses on the possibilities that I imagine as an educational leader for the future.

Acknowledgments

Writing a book is a journey that no one takes alone. This book has been in the making for a long time, ever since my days as a student and later as a classroom teacher. I owe a debt of gratitude to many people. They are too many to mention everyone. This is my first book and I could not have done it alone. This project would not have been possible without the support of family, friends, and colleagues who encouraged me to embark on this journey. Thanks to the many colleagues at the schools that I have worked, and colleagues in the academe who have supported and encouraged me to put my thoughts down in a book, and share my philosophy and ideas about the role of education in society. It has been a writing journey that has endured. I use the Peruvian quote "Little by Little One Walks Far" as a metaphor for my journey. It is a story of navigating unknown spaces as an outsider and immigrant while at the same time finding space to *be-come*, wrestling with the tensions of different cultures and worlds.

Thanks to my research participants who have graciously, and without hesitation, shared their narratives and stories. I hope that they will find this book useful as they continue their journey. It is also my hope that practitioners, and those who prepare leaders to work in schools, might find it useful. I owe a deep debt of gratitude to you. From you I have learned much. Without your stories this book would not have been possible and for that I am grateful. To my friends, I thank you all for your support. I will not list names as you are too many to name, but please know that you are all included, every one of you.

I would like to acknowledge my grandmother, Aggripine Heaven, affectionately called Mammy. My grandmother was my first teacher and instilled in me the value and joy of learning and discovering new ideas. She was everybody's grandmother, aunt, mother, and confidant. She was the most kind and caring human being that I have known. She believed in being socially just and modeled those values in her everyday life. Sankofa reminds us that we must go back and reclaim our past, so we can move forward and understand why and how we came to be who we are today. I will always draw on the knowledge and wisdom of my grandmother and ancestors, whose stories and narratives are truly empowering. My grandmother's narratives have persisted in my life and in my teaching. To my aunt Pam I offer a special acknowledgment for her unwavering support of family. I am grateful for her love and support. I am grateful for the love and support of my mom and dad, both of whom left us too young and too early. I know they are joyful of my accomplishments and are with me every step of the way. Thanks to my daughter, nephew, sisters, brother, aunts, uncles, and cousins. To my beautiful granddaughters Makaylah and Payton, you are the light and energy on my path.

I would also like to extend my appreciation to the editors at Palgrave Macmillan for their support and suggestions, and to my colleague and friend Donise Campbell-Scheffler who edited the final version of this book. I am thankful for their patience and understanding in seeing this project to the end.

My hope is that in some small way this book will be useful to educators who seek to create change in the lives of students, and in particular those who have been marginalized and underserved by the education system. For me it has been an amazing journey from a small town called Mt. Stewart in Westmoreland Jamaica, to the halls of the academy at the University of Toronto. I hope that my journey inspires other children no matter where they live or where they come from to dream, and to follow those dreams in charting new paths for themselves and others.

Contents

About the Author

Ann E. Lopez is currently a faculty member in the Department of Leadership, Higher and Adult Education at the Ontario Institute for Studies in Education/University of Toronto, Canada. Ann was born and raised in Jamaica and earned her doctorate from the University of Toronto in Curriculum Studies. Her doctoral research focused on Implementing Integrative Anti-Racist Curriculum: Negotiating Conflicts and Tensions Utilizing Experiential Collaborative Mentorship. Over the last 23 years Ann has held a variety of positions in public education. She is a former secondary classroom teacher and school administrator in one of the largest school boards in Canada. Ann most recently was the Academic Director of Initial Teacher Education at the University of Toronto where she collaboratively worked towards diversifying the teacher candidate pool. As Academic Director of Initial Teacher Education, Ann was responsible for both consecutive and concurrent teacher education programs, one of the largest teacher education programs in Canada.

Dr. Lopez's teaching and research focus on issues of equity, diversity, culturally responsive teaching, culturally responsive leadership, and social justice education, highlighting tensions involved in implementing critical practices, equity and diversity. Ann has presented her work and research at conferences in Canada, the Caribbean, Ghana, Kenya, Korea, and the United States. Ann's publications include *Critical perspectives in Diversity and Social Justice Education: Re-Conceptualizing Teacher Leadership Through Curriculum Inquiry in Pursuit of Social Justice: Case Study From the Canadian Context*. Dr. Lopez's articles have also appeared in journals such as *Multicultural Education Review*; *Mentoring and Tutoring: Partnership in Learning*; and *Canadian Journal of Educational Administration and Policy*.

Dr. Lopez is currently a Board member of the National Association for Multicultural Education (NAME) as well as the Regional Director for Region 8 and was recently elected President-Elect. Ann is a critical social justice educator who advocates for students who are not well served by the school system.

List of Figures

CHAPTER 1

Educational Realities and Current Context

All is not well in rapidly changing and transitioning schools as some teachers, administrators, and parents see their schools' increasing diversity as a problem instead of an opportunity for growth (Howard, 2007). Increasing diversity in schools is a phenomenon that cannot be ignored and presents significant challenges for teachers and educational leaders (Beachum & McCray, 2004). School leadership is difficult and complex (Bogotch & Reyes-Guerra, 2014) as demographic shifts have brought about greater diversity in Western countries. Populations have become more diverse ethnically, racially, and socially, as well as by sexual orientation, socio-economic status, physical abilities, languages spoken, and religion and other forms of social identity. Research suggests that the public and particularly diverse communities do not have confidence that public schools are serving the needs of culturally, ethnically, and linguistically diverse students (Nieto, 2004) who are fast becoming a large slice of the population in the public school system in the USA and other Western countries. Diversity and immigration is on the lips of everyone both on the "right" and the "left" of the political divide with differing viewpoints on ways that Western societies must respond to ensure greater inclusion, so that some people do not feel that they are permanently on the margins of society. The increased diversity in countries like Canada and the USA is an asset for growth, development and building bridges among different peoples of the world. It is important for a better world for people from different backgrounds to develop deeper understanding about each other.

A.E. Lopez, *Culturally Responsive and Socially Just Leadership in Diverse Contexts*, DOI 10.1057/978-1-137-53339-5_1

Immigrants also add to the growth of the economy by purchasing goods and services. The Ontario Trillium Foundation (2009/2010) noted that the growth of the immigrant and visible minority population shifted the makeup of Ontario's large urban centers and this has had an impact on growth. Pinar (2007) recognizing the value that diversity brings to society argues for *internationalization* that focuses on opportunities to become engaged with each other as we advance the values of peace, ecological sustainability and social justice.

All those involved in education must develop new approaches to schooling that respond to diversity in meaningful and practical ways so that students from diverse backgrounds can experience schooling positively. I hear stories often of how racialized students, poor students, students whose first language is not English are treated differently when it comes to discipline in school, lack of patience by some teachers whose tendency is to control and punish instead of employing culturally responsive approaches that connect with students and their experiences. My daughter who is an early childhood educator in Southern Ontario, said to me one day, "Mom, I had no idea these kids were beaten down and broken from kindergarten… I did not realize it until I was in the classroom on a regular basis…some teachers are great and love their job and the kids…others just complain about the kids and the communities they come from". I see Black and Brown students, especially boys being put on timeout more often and for longer periods, teachers using loud voices and an authoritarian approach to discipline when a gentle knudge would suffice".

In Canada by 2031 between 25 % and 28 % of the population could be foreign-born and 47 % of second-generation Canadians (Canadian-born children of immigrants) will belong to a visible minority group. The Canadian Employment Equity Act defines visible minorites as "persons other than Aboriginal persons, who are non-Caucasian in race or non-White in color". I acknowledge that the term visible minority is a contested term as some argue that it futhers the marginalization of racialized Canadians. As well 29 % to 32 % of the population or between 11.4 and 14.4 million people could belong to a visible minority group (Statistics Canada, 2011). This is more than double the number (5.3 million) reported in 2006. In the USA the trend is much the same. By 2044, more than half of all Americans are projected to belong to a minority group (any group other than non-Hispanic White alone), and by 2060, nearly one in five of the nation's total population is projected to be foreign born (US Department of Commerce, 2015). By 2024, the number of White students enrolled in public schools is projected to decrease. Their share of enrollment is expected to decline and to be less than 50 % beginning in 2014. The enrollment of Hispanic students and Asian/Pacific Islander students is expected to increase. The number of Hispanic public school students is projected to increase from 12.5 million in 2013 to 15.5 million in 2024 and represent 29 % of total enrollment (U.S. Department of Education Institute of Education Sciences National Center for Education Statistics, 2015). This will be the new reality in schools.

This increasing diversity poses new challenges as well as opportunities for educators and policy makers. Educators must embrace the richness that diversity brings and the possibilities of gaining new understanding to inform their practice. Parents and students from diverse communities expect that their children will be given opportunities to succeed in school. This means education that reflects their experiences and not steeped in the discourses, knowledge and practices of the dominant. Students must be able to see themselves in the curriculum, the teaching staff and school administration. Diversity offers opportunities for transfomative leaderhip in schools. Transformative leadership is based on dialogue and strong relationships with communities-it is a leadership approach that is socially just and deeply democratic (Shields, 2010). When communities are involved in the education process at all levels, the learning experiences of students are enhanced. The challenge of the 21st Century is to create schools that ensure that all students in all communities are succeeding (Darling-Hammond, 1997). Communities are no longer homogenous; they are a combination of different peoples with different experiences that must find ways to coexist respectfully inside and outside of schools. With the projected changes in the population, it is undeniable that the fabric of society in Western countries as we know it is changing. In recent years there have been vigorous debates in North America and other Western countries on the impact of this demographic shift and immigration on society and education. Schools cannot function as they have done in the past. They must find a different purpose than when they were structured to teach order and conformity to the elite group (Tyack, 1974). Preparing students from communities that are more diverse than ever before looks much different today, as their experiences are different and technology provides students access to more information (Hargreaves & Fullan, 1998). The changes that are taking place in schools as a result of increased immigration, in addition to the demands for educational reform and accountability, create challenges for school leaders all over

(White & Cooper, 2012). Theorists such as Gloria Ladson-Billings, Maxine Green and others call on educational leaders, researchers and school-based scholars to understand the soocioeconomic and hegemonic power that schools have on how society is organized and the important role for social justice leadership in this context (Lopez, 2014). Canada is known for multiculturalism and diversity, yet homelessness and poverty still exist, particularly among Aboriginal communities, racialized and low-income populations (Lopez, 2014). A report by the Ontario Black Educators Network reveals that despite the growing diversity in Ontario's classrooms, teachers and administrators do not fully reflect the background of those in the classroom (Turner, 2015).

Research continues to show that many students from diverse communities and backgrounds, racialized students, and Aboriginal students are not achieving in school in the same way as their White counterparts. Over recent decades reformers have created and redesigned thousands of schools that are educating students from different racial, social, economic, and cultural backgrounds; however these schools and students remain at the margin of the educative process (Darling-Hammond, 1997). Scholars such as (Dei, Mazzuca, McIsaac, & Zine, 1997; James & Brathwaite, 1996) over the years have documented the plight of Black students, particularly Black boys in the Canadian education system. According to Dei (2015), students of color continue to underachieve and feel disengaged from the school system. I argue that students are not broken and in need of fixing but rather the school system needs to adjust to their needs, realities, and experiences. School leaders in the study spoke of challenges they faced advocating for students from diverse communities whose educational needs they believe are not being met. For example, some teachers are sometimes unwilling to acknowledge that change is needed in their pedagogy and curriculum. The urgent need for culturally responsive practices to be embedded in teaching, discipline, and other aspects of schooling has never been greater. The *US News and World Report* (2015) noted that American education is rife with problems, starting with the gaping differences between White students and students of color. The American Psychological Association (2012) reports that ongoing ethnic and racial disparities in education in the USA follow a pattern in which African American, American Indian, Latino, and Southeast Asian groups underperform academically, relative to Whites and other Asian Americans. The disparity in educational outcomes for marginalized and racialized students cannot continue if our societies are to move forward. The great educator and philosopher John Dewey argued that the responsibility of educators is to support students in seeing that education is important to them and their ability to contribute to society. Educators must push back at the demonization of immigrants that is currently occurring in public discourse. They must continue to work towards greater equity in education where all students have the opportunity to be successful. It is imperative that students no matter their background feel included, are engaged in the education system, and achieve success. Dei and Doyle-Woods (2009) call for educators to be brave and respond to difference and diversity within the schooling population, ensuring that curriculum, pedagogy, and texts reflect the diverse knowledge, experiences of students' histories, ideas, lived experiences, and struggles.

The role of the school leader in this context is to advocate on behalf of students, increase their awareness of oppression, subvert dominant paradigms, and commit to advocate for educational change on behalf of traditionally oppressed and marginalized students (Jean-Marie, Normore, & Brooks, 2009). Leadership and its role in the achievement of students is an area that is still developing. There are various typologies of leadership and some argue that what leadership is and how it is defined continues to be an elusive concept (Leo & Barton, 2006). However, educational leaders in all areas of the education system have a role to play in these ever-changing and diverse contexts. Most people care about schools because their children attend and they believe that the country's future depends upon children attending public schools and getting an education (Reagle, 2006).

Challenges and Possibilities for School Leaders in the Face of Growing Diversity

School leaders are not a homogenous group. They come from different ethnicities and racial groups. They also have fluid and intersecting identities, bringing varying experiences to their leadership roles that impact their work in diverse contexts in different ways. These differences create complexities that call for deeper understanding of the issues as well as possibilities for action. Diversity cannot and should not be essentialized, and the complexity of the issue must be acknowledged. There isn't a one-size-fits-all solution to issues of diversity. For example, some school leaders who are White might need training and support on ways to respond to Aboriginal, Black, and Brown students-how to respectfully border-cross across cultures. Similarly some Black educators might need to develop deeper understanding of how to work with Latino/a students more effectively. Some school leaders might also have to learn more effective ways of supporting students from ethnic backgrounds where "positive stereotypes" and "inflated expectations" that impact those students negatively are challenged. Scholars such as (Chou, 2008 ; Yeh, 2001; Yin, 2000) and others argue that the model minority stereotype attributes educational and economic success to Asian Americans, and ignores the challenges that these students face such as poverty and language barriers. In Canada, some South Asians have expressed similar concerns (see Navaratnam, 2011).

One of the many challenges facing school leaders is how to translate their theory of understanding into practice. That is, implementing practices that treat diversity as an asset and as an important ingredient in preparing students for a world that is rapidly changing, without essentializing their experiences. By not addressing the needs of the growing diverse student population, schools contribute to high dropout rates and disengagement of students (McMahon & Portelli, 2004). Some argue that cultural diversity in schools is not taken into account enough as an important variable in the personal and social development of students (Aguado, Ballesteros, & Malik, 2002) and this runs the risk of thwarting their social development. Funding cuts, limited resources, neo-liberal reforms, and increasing demands make the work of educational leaders more challenging. Educators are frustrated that there is a lot of talk about diversity, but there seems to be slow progress made in reducing the achievement gap between the educational haves and the have-nots (Darling-Hammond, 2011). The US Department of Education recently called for more emphasis on equity in funding educational opportunities (Equity and Excellence Commission, 2013).

School leaders must not only think of ways to implement practices that are equitable and culturally responsive and seize upon the potential that diversity offers, they must also challenge dominant discourses and knowledge that have dominated education for centuries. Bogotch (2014) suggests that educational leaders must engage the dominant discourse in ways that disrupt the status quo. This is an ongoing journey of adjusting, re-thinking, creating new epistemologies, and seeking out possibilities for action. Bogotch and Shields (2014) argue that educational leadership is still dominated by technical approaches to efficiency and effectiveness, and that leadership for social justice must be deliberately focused on disturbing and disrupting conventional wisdom and dominant school practices. It is important for the well-being and educational outcome of students, and in particular diverse students, that school leaders have a framework for reflection and action that guides their work articulating a philosophy - being purposeful in approach and actions that reflect this philosophy. In addition to identifying some of the challenges that educational leaders face in schools today, this book suggests ways that school leaders can engage in culturally responsive and socially just leadership practices.

It is important that we examine critical approaches to educational leadership that challenge hegemonic notions and practices of education, while at the same time articulating actions that will bring about change in the lives of diverse students and those who have been traditionally underserved and marginalized. From a leadership perspective, progressive leadership theories such as culturally responsive leadership and social justice leadership are seen as viable ways of bringing about change. These frameworks will be further explored in Chap. 2 however as Theoharis (2007) suggests leadership grounded in social justice must address the daily realities of school. Theoharis argues further that those who embrace social justice leadership must "make issues of race, class, gender, disability, sexual orientation, and other historically and currently marginalizing conditions … central to their advocacy, leadership practice, and vision … that centers on addressing and eliminating marginalization in schools" (p. 223). As I have suggested before the kind of leadership that is employed in schools is important in ensuring that the educational needs of diverse students are met. This includes leadership at all levels - teachers and administrators. However, as I have seen from my own experiences as a classroom teacher and school administrator, those in leadership positions at the administrative level can play an important role in supporting teachers, create environments that are responsive to diverse students, allocate resources to support programs, and support parents and communities. Some argue that school administrators bear great responsibility in hiring and retaining teachers who are capable of working in diverse contexts and with marginalized populations, working collaboratively to bring about change. The principalship is often recognized in schools as the office where the "buck stops" and principals are given enormous power to run their schools. Principals are held accountable for progress of students, and must develop the goals and the vision that guide their schools (Leithwood & Jantzi, 2006). The principalship is the most identifiable leadership position in schools empowered by district policy (Khalifa, Gooden, & Davis, 2016) and has great influence. The same could be said in Ontario where principals have enormous power under the Education Act. Given the importance of the principalship how those aspiring to be principals are prepared must become of a focus of scholars and researchers advocating for culturally responsive and social justice leadership.

My time spent as a school administrator in two large diverse schools in the Greater Toronto Area has allowed me see firsthand the importance of embedding issues of diversity and equity in the work of school leaders at all levels, but most importantly at the administrator level and in educational leadership as a whole. We know from research that when the various and multiple identities of students (ethnicity, race, language, religion, sexual orientation, gender, social class, or other forms of identity) are taken into account their chances of success improve. In most schools in the Western world students of color, female students, poor students, students who identify as gay, lesbian, or transgendered, and students with physical disabilities do not have the same positive experiences at school as their White able-bodied counterparts. Educational leaders have a role and responsibility to work for change in these contexts. Gunter (2006) suggests that educational leaders when examining how to deal with the challenges that diversity poses must look at how categories are produced and "tunnel beneath the logic of othering" (p. 262). Gunter argues further there is need for "reconceptualizing the school within the public domain, and how this makes statements for how we want to live together. The existence of public sector schools assumes that we care about those who we are not genetically connected to, but we also have to note that there are those who engage in practice and support arguments which suggest that they do not care, and as such the state involvement in schooling may not be as secure as we might assume" (p. 262/266). Those who work with culturally diverse students have an ethical and moral responsibility to take engage in leadership practices that challenge taken-for-granted approaches that exclude the voices and experiences of some students (Lopez, 2014). Social justice leaders must acknowledge the challenges and possibilities that confront us as educators today and act.

When School Leaders Deal with Issues of Diversity It Benefits Everyone—"That's Just Good Leadership"

In imploring teachers to teach in ways that are culturally responsive Ladson-Billings (1995b) argues that culturally relevant pedagogy is good teaching that all teachers should embrace. Her ideas and notions of culturally responsive teaching are amplified in her seminal work "But That's Just Good Teaching". In the same vein I believe when school leaders engage in social justice and culturally responsive leadership, "That's Just Good Leadership". Leadership that is inclusive, challenges the status quo, and responds to diverse learners benefits all students and is good leadership. It is not asking leaders to engage in practices that are not within their ability. According to Dei (2000), when educators examine how various forms of difference impact students they are better able to understand factors that influence students' learning, engagement, and disengagement with school. Reconceptualizing educational aims and objectives that take into account diversity and all forms of difference is important in creating schools that are inclusive (Dei, James, Karumanchery, James-Wilson, & Zine, 2000). As Foster (1989) argues leadership must be analyzed through the political-historical lens which is about examining politics and power. School leaders play an important role in transforming the social context of diverse students and in so doing must examine the politics of schooling and how power is used to oppress and marginalize.

Sometimes when issues of diversity and equity are raised, some teachers, students, and school leaders feel that the issue is not of concern to them, but primarily for people of color and those who live in urban areas, or suggest that issues of equity and diversity have been solved and we should move on. We know from experience and research that this is not the case. We also know that when those who are at the margins do better, society as a whole is lifted up. Even though there is more work to be done, some countries like Canada are making strides in dealing with issues of equity and diversity in schools. A report by the Organization for Economic Cooperation and Development (2012) noted that in Canada public schools do a better job than those of almost all other countries in equalizing opportunities between economically advantaged and disadvantaged students. Recent report by the Peel District School Board (2016) on their Action Plan to Support Black Male Students creates cause for hope. This focuses on four key areas: Engagement with community, Anti-racism professional development, Integration of the experiences of Black Canadians in the curriculum, and inspiring Black student leadership and engagement. A commitment to excellence and equity has been central to the advances made in education in the USA, and societal progress is contingent upon expanding opportunities for all (Blankstein & Noguera, 2015). When educational leaders address issues of diversity, they inevitably challenge forms of difference such as ageism, ability, classism, racism, sexual orientation, and other factors that define who we are. In the twenty-first century, demography does not have to determine destiny and students' identities do not have to be seen as separate from their educational advancement (Blankstein & Noguera, 2015).

I believe that in Canada we have made some progress from the times when Patrick Solomon (1995b, 1997) asserted that the perspectives and practices of Canadian educators were resistant to cultural pluralism and antiracist education in classrooms. There is greater tolerance now, as school boards and the Ontario Ministry of Education have policies on equity and diversity that are referred to in mission statements. However, school leaders and teachers advocating for more culturally responsive and socially just approaches have argued that change has been slow on the ground in addressing the challenges that diverse students face. In 2009 the Ontario government released the Ontario Equity and Inclusive Strategy. The Strategy gave prominence to issues of equity in education in Ontario. It was introduced to give educators at all levels a framework to engage in equity education. Some have argued that while this was a good start, more needs to be done to hold schools and school boards accountable on implementation of the policy. Ontario's Premier Kathleen Wynne noted:

> Embracing diversity and moving beyond tolerance to acceptance and respect will help us reach our goal of making Ontario's education system the most inclusive in the world. We believe – and research confirms – that students who feel welcome and accepted in their schools are more likely to succeed academically. We believe that everyone in our publicly funded education system – regardless of background or personal circumstances – must be welcomed and accepted, and thereby enabled to reach their highest potential (p. 1).

Of note is the desire and stated objective to move beyond tolerance to acceptance. It is important for educators to tease out what are acceptable practices of acceptance and how these can be implemented. The Ontario Equity and Inclusive Strategy states that:

> Education directly influences students' life chances – and life outcomes. Today's global, knowledge-based economy makes the ongoing work in our schools critical to our students' success in life and to Ontario's economic

> future. As an agent of change and social cohesion, our education system supports and reflects the democratic values of fairness, equity, and respect for all. The schools we create today will shape the society that we, and our children share tomorrow (p. 5).

In 2014 the Ontario Equity and Inclusive Strategy was revisited and Ontario's diversity foregrounded. It was noted that addressing diversity in schools is important to the overall success of the society as a whole. It stated:

> Ontario's diversity is one of its greatest assets – both today and for the future. Embracing this diversity and moving beyond tolerance and celebration to inclusivity and respect will help us reach our goal of making Ontario's education system the most equitable in the world. Everyone in our publicly funded education system – regardless of background or personal circumstances – must feel engaged and included. Realizing the promise of our diversity is a continuous process grounded in actively respecting and valuing the full range of our differences. Providing a high-quality education for all is a key means of fostering social cohesion, within an inclusive society where diversity is affirmed in a framework of common values that promote the well-being of all citizens (p. 6).

It is time to move beyond tolerance and laminated forms of equity and social justice where statements about equity are framed in plastic covers and placed on walls in schools in the front office, often for parents and students to see, but nothing changes in the experiences of diverse students (Lopez, 2006, 2013). In many instances the staff and administration remain predominantly White, the curriculum is dotted with references to diverse peoples, but not much else changes. Within the context of the Ontario Equity and Inclusive Strategy (2014) there are special guidelines for educational leaders at all levels. School leaders are charged with promoting the development of collaborative environments and ensuring that student achievement remains a high priority within a culture of high expectations. However, there is still much work to be done to realize the promise of Ontario's Equity and Inclusive Strategy. This is one of the conundrums of educational leadership—how to translate well-meaning policies like the Ontario Equity and Inclusive Strategy into meaningful action on the ground in schools and classrooms.

It is not easy challenging the status quo. Educational leaders who seek to disrupt existing ways of doing and knowing are often faced with resistance. School leaders, whose narratives and experiences inform this book, highlight the resistance that they experienced in schools, from teachers suggesting that there is no need to focus on diversity as everyone is "equal" to outright lack of cooperation. The kind of leadership that is needed to bring about deep, lasting, and sustained change in the lives of students who have been traditionally underserved and who underachieve in schools must be dauntless in the face of resistance. Society as a whole will benefit from an improved educational system. This means that educators must take conscious actions and engage in practices that strengthen diverse students and their communities. According to Blankstein and Noguera (2015) equity is premised upon the recognition that all children have different identities and lived experiences and there must be a commitment to meet the needs of all students so that they can grow up and have a successful life. This requires leadership that is dauntless, fearless and individuals who are willing to take risks on behalf of students. Leaders must foreground diversity and equity in discernable actions and practices. In keeping with Foster (1989) this kind of leadership is s form of critical practice that rejects a managerial approach to leadership and is more than "how to manuals" that are prepared for aspiring leaders. The nature of leadership in schools must change so that so much time is not spent on the day to day managerial aspects of the job, but more time is spent on working with students and teachers. Principals' everyday practices do not fall into neat litte boxes, each day they must navigate competing priorities. According to Tompson (2001) the role of the principal is messy and eological - holistic, unpredictable, consumig and contradictory, pulling in all directions at once.

Dauntless leadership re-imagines culturally responsive leadership that is focused on challenging practices that reproduce dominant values, and ways of knowing that marginalize some students based on class, race, sexual orientation, language, immigrant status, and so on. According to the Merriam-Webster dictionary, a person who is dauntless is fearless and determined. Dauntless leaders fight for change in the face of resistance, and seek ways to sustain themselves on the journey, and turn resistance into possibilities (Lopez, 2015). This dauntless and fearless leadership that I suggest is grounded in the work of school leaders and practitioners as evidenced by the participants in the study. It is a vision of educational leadership that can be realized through values, beliefs, and actions (Walker & Dimmock, 2005).

Change will not be sustained in any school if the community, teaching staff, and all stakeholders do not buy in. This means that those involved in this kind of equity and social justice work must also seek to build bridges with others and boldly cross borders into spaces that they might not be familiar with. In much the same way that professional learning communities come together in schools to look at issues such as assessment and evaluation, literacy and other system-wide initiatives, these same learning communities must come together around issues of equity and diversity that move beyond "multicultural days" and superficial cultural feel good events. They must ask tough questions about the plight of those who are underachieving, why they are underachieving, and what can be done. The challenges in education are great and this work will go on for a very long time. In this book I am not advocating ideas that have not been thought about before; what I am positing and adding to the discourse are additional examples and ways in which these goals can be achieved, and, as Marshall (2004) suggests, not only to change schools, but also society as well.

Think Alouds—Questions for Reflection

1. What is the demographic composition of your school or board? How has your school changed demographically over the years?
2. How have school leaders in your school or district responded to the growing diversity in the school community? Provide some examples.
3. What are some of the challenges that you have faced in implementing equity initiatives and policies in your school or district?
4. How would you describe your own leadership practice? What else might you need to learn about ways that you can effectively serve the needs of diverse students?
5. What do you see as some of the inherent tensions of the rapid demographic shift that has taken place globally?

Research Activity

1. Research and review the evolution of educational leadership theories and educational administration over the last twenty five years. What are the changes that have been advanced in this typology on the ways that leadership is understood and practised in schools today?
2. How might notions of critical practice inform your leadership philosophy? What are some of the challenges for school leaders in an era of accountablity and limited resources?

CHAPTER 2

Toward a Theory of Culturally Responsive and Social Justice Leadership

The importance of school leaders in responding to the demands of 21st Century education, that focuses on raising achievement for all students and the quality of education, is without question. Researchers and policy makers must understand the effects, roles, and responsibilities of educational leaders in a time of tremendous demographic shifts and recognize diversity as a major contributor to educational change (Goodard, Neumerski, Goddard, Salloum, & Berebitsking, 2010). School leaders are under tremendous pressure to respond to the growing diversity in schools reflected in the social changes that are taking place in society. Schools are cultural spaces where dialogue and discourse occur and represent the contradictions of society, where understandings and meanings are teased out at the same time tensions are explored. Scholars such as Di Paola, Tarter, and Hoy (2005); Horsford (2010) suggest that schools are contradictory spaces where harmony coexists with conflict. In this milieu there have been calls for the learning environment in schools to be more responsive to the needs of diverse learners (Howard, 2003). In this chapter I elucidate the tenets of culturally responsive leadership and social justice leadership as workable theoretical frameworks for school leaders. I agree with Bogotch and Shields (2014) who contend that leadership is still dominated by technical approaches of efficiency and effectiveness and who argue that educational leadership for social justice must be deliberately focused on disturbing conventional wisdom and dominant school practices. Smyth

A.E. Lopez, *Culturally Responsive and Socially Just Leadership in Diverse Contexts*, DOI 10.1057/978-1-137-53339-5_2

(1989) suggests that leadership must enable all voices to be heard regardless of class, race, gender or postion in the formal hiearchy of the school.

One of the challenges for educational leaders is improving the school climate and culture so that students with multiple and shifting identities can find themselves within it. Researchers and practitioners are embracing a more dynamic view of culture that is fluid, and encompasses all aspects of emergent global identities, multiplicities of identities, and experiences that comprise today's youth culture (Ladson-Billings, 2014; Paris & Alim, 2014). There are cultural differences among students that must be bridged and cross-cultural understanding developed. Paris (2012) describes this as cultural pluralism. It is important that educational leaders develop understanding across cultures and are able to border cross between cultures. As educators, we must recognize that our varying experiences as human beings are constructed within fluid and moving cultures. According to Ladson-Billings (2014) culture is an amalgamation of human activity, production, thought, belief systems, norms, and customs that are not static, but always changing. Understanding that culture is fluid, and that people come to understand and define their own culture is important for those who embrace theoretical frameworks that are culturally responsive and socially just. Brayboy (2005) argues that culture as a concept is simultaneously fluid and dynamic, and sometimes fixed. For diverse and immigrant students their racial identity and home country experiences might be fixed, while at the same time they are gaining new cultures in their new learning spaces and home. Culture can also be rooted in resistance, is political, and focuses on peoples' shared beliefs and behaviors that distinguish them from others and at the same time offer a sense of shared meaning (Borofsk, Barth, Schweda, Rodseth, & Stolzenberg, 2001). These ontologies are important for diverse students in multicultural Western societies and directly connect to their identity as they try to blend home and school community cultures. We must however be careful that we do not set up dichotomies between different aspect of identities such as disability cultures, global cultures, and so on, as this approach fails to realize that school culture cannot be disconnected from community and global culture and risk reducing students to a single monolithic culture which is neither relevant nor realistic (Vassallo, 2015).

I see culturally responsive leadership and social justice leadership as intertwined and overlapping notwithstanding subtle differences in ways that scholars articulate their theoretical framing. Culturally responsive and socially just leaders challenge all forms of oppression, influence the contexts in which they work, and ultimately the lives of students. These contexts include not only the classrooms, the halls, and the front office, but also how decisions are made around issues such as the allocation of resources and the level of community involvement. It is the entire milieu from the moment students walk into the school that some argue, in fact, is what embodies the curriculum. Allingham (1992) noted:

> Curriculum includes texts and storybooks; pictures displayed; classroom seating plans; group work; posters; music; announcements; prayers and readings; languages spoken in the school; food served in the cafeteria; visitors invited to the classrooms; reception offered to parents in the office; racial make-up of the office staff, the custodial staff, teachers, and administration; displays of student work; makeup of school teams; sports played; clubs; school logo emblem; field trips; assignments and projects; facial expressions and body language; clothes worn,...in short, the whole environment (p. 5).

In this environment educational leaders are called on to reframe the social discourse by examining their unconscious frames of reference, becoming aware and then using a new language and new points of view to modify their cultural models. Leaders must also take action toward conscious engagement (Lewison, Leland, & Harste, 2007).

Culturally Responsive Leadership

Culturally responsive leadership builds on culturally responsive and culturally relevant pedagogical theories (Gay, 2000; Ladson-Billings, 1995b) that focus on teaching which includes the cultural experiences of students while raising their understanding of the importance of social critique and inclusive curriculum through which they achieve academic success. Educators who advocate for culturally responsive pedagogy argue that people learn differently across cultures. In order to maximize learning opportunities, teachers must gain knowledge of the cultures represented in their classrooms and then translate this knowledge into instructional practice (Villegas, 1991). Ladson-Billings (1995a) theorizes culturally responsive pedagogy as a pedagogy of opposition, committed to collective and individual empowerment of students. This pedagogy also challenges students to critically examine society and to work for social change. The core principles of culturally responsive theory revolve around academic success, development of cultural competence, and socio-political and critical consciousness. Banks and Banks (1995) remind us that students need to develop literacy, numeracy, and technological skills in ways that are relevant to their lives. Cultural competence is a vehicle for learning where students see their identities and cultures as strengths. Culturally relevant teaching advocates for students to hold on to their cultural integrity while achieving academic excellence where their cultures become vehicles for learning (Ladson-Billings, 1995b). Culturally relevant teaching is not an add-on it must be embedded and woven into the curriculum. When students develop socio-political consciousness, they are able to critique the cultural norms and values of institutions that produce and maintain social inequities (Lopez, 2011). For diverse students to thrive in schools it is important that dominant ways of knowing and the knowledge of minority students are constructed in a new respectful reality (Nieto, 2004). Culturally responsive pedagogy supports the acculturation of students that constructs new dynamics instead of assimilation that subsumes their identities to that of the dominant. Acculturation creates environments where teachers and students co-construct new knowledge with deep respect. Critical educators theorize schooling as part of the struggle for democracy and social justice that not only highlights the issues to be challenged, but engages in productive dialogue and action (Freire, 1998; Kincheloe & McLaren, 2008). If we are to move forward in reconstructing a socially just education and society, we must learn from the experiences of those who have been on the margins. Culturally responsive leadership builds on these notions of culturally responsive pedagogy that broaden understanding beyond the classroom per se to the larger school milieu and decision-making in schools.

Like culturally responsive teaching and culturally responsive pedagogy there are many approaches to culturally responsive leadership that focus on different aspects of leadership, interpretations, and theorizing (see Gooden, 2005; Gooden & Dantley, 2012; Johnson, 2014; Khalifa, 2013; Lopez, 2015, 2016a; Madhlangobe & Gordon, 2012; Ryan, 2015). Freire (1970) brought to the world of education the notion that oppressed people could and should take matters in their own hands if they want change and urged learners to engage in *conscientization* that is, challenging the systems and structures that oppress them, to see students not as empty vessels to be filled with knowledge, but as people with knowledge to offer. I argue for culturally responsive leadership that builds on the notion of *conscientization*, a form of activism, that provides a way for educational leaders to theorize their work, develop agency, take action, and build schoolwide capacity on issues of equity, diversity, and social justice (Lopez, 2015). Through deep self-reflection leaders examine their practices and make a commitment to learn new leadership epistemologies of resistance. Educational leaders must be prepared to understand how their work, advocacy, and agenda for social justice education are important aspects of their professional capital (Murakami-Ramalho & Pankake, 2012). I believe that culturally responsive leadership is an effective leadership theory that practitioners can utilize to bring about change.

Beachum (2011) suggests key tenets of culturally responsive leadership that I share: (1) the development of emancipatory consciousness that focuses on educators' awareness of the history and detrimental impact of societal inequities; (2) equitable insights that focus on the development of attitudes that promote inclusion throughout the school community; and (3) engagement in reflexive practices whereby educators critically examine the work that they do. School leaders promote culturally responsive leadership by demonstrating culturally responsive approaches themselves as leaders in their relations with the community, colleagues, and students (Riehl, 2000). The goal of culturally responsive leadership is to create structures and environments for others to experience the freedom to become their best selves (Davis, 2002). According to Davis:

> When we talk about culturally responsive leadership we are really talking about acknowledging the need for educational leaders to value unconditionally the students they serve. This stems from the fundamental belief in the idea that students are a wealth of prior knowledge about their world from which educators can create and support meaningful educational experiences ... if we are to create systems that can enrich the lives of poor and minority children, we must develop a philosophy of leadership that is mindful of the importance and significance of culture ... culturally responsive leadership is essentially a process by which we can create systems that support democratic education (p. 5).

In positing culturally responsive leadership as a workable solution, I envision the philosophy, values, commitment, and focused actions of educational leaders in a connected loop of key leadership processes and actions to transform (Lopez, 2015). Philosophy and values without actions to implement and influence is akin to inert knowledge, which is information and knowledge that one has, but does not use.

Culturally responsive leadership is critical leadership that argues for continued analysis of what occurs in an organization with a commitment by those involved to engage in critical reflection and re-evaluation of current practices (Foster, 1989). Educational leaders who ground their work in critical perspectives seek to create social change by challenging the status quo and systems of power that dominate and subjugate. The challenge has always been how to translate this ideology and perspective into practice. Foster (1986) argues that moving the agenda along and disrupting practices that exclude requires educational leaders to develop understandings of how people and positions are involved in running a school. This is the theory to practice dilemma (praxis) that is so crucial and is talked about constantly in education in areas such as teacher education and principal preparation programs. It is important for school leaders to move beyond theorizing. For school-based scholars (Lopez, 2014), it is important to ask—what does this look like in my daily life as a school leader? How do I go about changing existing conditions? What are the kinds of support and resoiurces that I might need? How do I influence policy so that it reflects the needs of diverse learners and their communities? Jean-Marie and Normore (2010) suggest that it is important for educators to tease out the work involved in a critical model of leadership so that others can learn from it. Leadership that is critical must break away from the discourse of standardization that is taking over the educational discourse in the USA and elsewhere. Some suggest that standardization will improve the quality of education even though research shows the contrary.

In Ontario, Canada, we have had our experiences in the nineties with the election of a Conservative government in the 1990's that called for educational reforms including teacher testing and funding based on balancing the budget instead of the needs of students. Under the slogan of a "common sense revolution" the Conservative government at the time restructured education in Ontario and many of the programs that worked toward equity and social justice were severely cut back or terminated, and racial, gender, and cultural minorities found themselves on the receiving end of the conservative agenda (Dehli, 1996). I recall walking the sidewalk as a fairly new teacher as teachers went on strike against the Conservative government's Bill 160. The Bill sought to strip away the independence of teachers and reduce the impact of unions at the administrator level. Notwithstanding the protests of the teachers' unions Bill 160 was eventually passed and school administrators were removed from unions. Up until that time teachers and school administrators belonged to the same union. The impact of that change on school leadership in Ontario schools was profound as school administrators for a while were no longer seen as natural partners in a collaborative teaching and learning process, but more as managers. The rhetoric of the Ontario government at the time reflected a neo-conservative spin on efficiency and accountability, and the need to reinstate the management functions of school administrators. Additionally, the Conservative government enacted budgets that saw major cuts to education and how schools were funded. The impact of the cuts imposed dealt an enormous blow to the future of antiracist education in Ontario as "they directly opposed initiatives that worked toward ameliorating the problems of representation on schooling" (Dei, Karumanchery, & Leeno, 1999, p. 6). Bill 160, the cornerstone of the conservative education legislative agenda, was buttressed by a business model that placed decision-making in the hands of a few under the guise of a reform and accountability agenda. Those who argue for culturally responsive and socially just leadership practices challenge this notion of school leadership, believe that it is reactionary and does not support the teaching and learning of students. Dantley (1990) argues that critical leadership focuses on persistent dialogue, collaboration, political and social change, where schools become spaces for critical thought and reflection, engagement in critical pedagogy that facilitates critical reflexive thinking, and where schools serve as the preparatory arenas for political and social change. Critical leaders must be transformative through activism and creativity and search for possibilities that respond to difference and diversity.

Change is not easy, but culturally responsive leaders and social justice leaders must seek out space in the education system where they can work towards change. In Ontario for example, culturally responsive school leaders are encouraged to examine ways that they might be able to advance their work within the context of the Ontario Leadership Framework. The Ontario Leadership Framework (OLF) is used by school boards in the province as the current model to guide effective school leadership and to prepare those who are aspiring to be school administrators. Within the Ontario context it is important that critical educational leaders examine the OLF for ways that it can best respond to the needs of diverse students, by looking at what is missing and positing ways that it can be enhanced. OLF was introduced in 2006 by the Ministry of Education to influence leadership practices in Ontario. It was created to act as the "foundation for all aspects of the Ontario Leadership Strategy" (OLS) (Ontario, 2010c, p. 6). The OLS was developed as a "long term systematic leadership development initiative" that was formed on the notion that "school leadership, especially by the principal is second only to teaching in terms of the impact in student learning" (Ontario, 2010c, p. 3). It was launched by the Premier of Ontario in 2008 and has become the Ministry of Education's conceptual framework for leadership development in Ontario. The Ontario Leadership Framework (2013) is designed to:

- Facilitate a shared vision of leadership in schools and districts.
- Promote a common language that fosters an understanding of leadership and what it means to be a school or system leader.
- Identify the practices, actions, and traits or personal characteristics that describe effective leadership.
- Guide the design and implementation of professional learning and development for school and system leaders.
- Identify the characteristics of high-performing schools and systems—K-12 school.
- School Effectiveness Framework (SEF) and District Effectiveness Framework (DEF).
- Aid in the recruitment, development, selection, and retention of school and system leaders.

The OLF, I believe, provides school leaders with an opportunity to look for ways to be creative and to act boldly on behalf of diverse students. For example, insisting that a critical approach to diversity is taken when shared vision is being discussed in schools and questioning the theoretical frames that undergird the understanding of leadership. If school leaders claim to be culturally responsive and socially just they must be able to articulate what that means in their context and what actions they hope to pursue. Professional learning and development must include critical approaches to diversity but it is important to determine how will this be included in professional development and training for school leaders. Practising school leaders who embrace critical approaches must always ask what might this look like in action? How does the idea of culturally responsive leadeship translates in this context? How will the impact of the actions taken be measured? How are school and school boards held accountable to ensure that culturally responsive and social justice goals so often expressed in mission statemennts become reality? How will training and development be implemented? As far as diversity is concerned, the OLF acknowledges that diversity is important and contextual. It states that:

> Successful school and system leaders must be responsive to the diverse nature of Ontario's communities. The OLF describes leadership broadly in a way that

> is intended to be inclusive of the diversity found in schools and communities across the province. Application of the OLF should be shaped by the community context... The demographic and contextual diversity in Ontario schools, together with the province's commitment to high levels of student achievement and well-being, have heightened the importance of effective leadership in schools and districts led by leaders who support diverse student needs by providing caring, safe, respectful and engaging learning environments (p. 9).

School leaders who advocate for critical action must be watchdogs in the system to ensure that promises are kept. Ryan (2015) calls this strategic activism and suggests that educational leaders must "understand their political environments and how they think about strategizing" (p. 3). While Ryan recognizes that activism is challenging for school leaders and is a complex endeavor, he reminds educational leaders that activism need not be aggressive, glamorous, or spectacular. Activism it can be simple acts such as facilitating a workshop for teachers where the focus is on improving equity in the school, ensuring that parents have the required information to be fully involved, or supporting each other by sharing resources.

Culturally Responsive Leadership Model

Many school leaders ask: how do I begin the journey of culturally responsive leadership? I suggest the model below as one way that educators can begin to think about practical steps in that direction. Culturally responsive leaders are encouraged to acquire critical approaches in their work that centers diversity and difference (Cochran-Smith, Davis, & Fries, 2004; Nieto, 2004). Culturally responsive leadership demands courage, taking risks, journeying, dealing with tensions, developing agency, and deep critical reflection. Drawing on my earlier collaborative action research with teachers implementing culturally responsive practices (Lopez, 2005, 2011), my most recent research with educational leaders (Lopez, 2015, 2016b), and critical educational leadership literature, I suggest the model below of culturally responsive leadership built on pillars of critical examination, reflection, collaboration, and agency. I suggest that critical leadership begins with examination of self. In this critical stance, leaders examine their own positionality, their cultures and values, and how these are mediated in diverse learning spaces. This model aligns with Beachum's (2011) tenets of culturally responsive leadership that call for culturally responsive leaders to examine the development of emancipatory consciousness that focuses on educators' awareness of history, and the detrimental impact of societal inequities. Beachum calls for educators to engage in reflexive practices whereby they critically examine the work that they do. To change the experiences of diverse students, school leaders and diverse students must co-construct knowledge that reflects the complex contexts in which they teach and learn.

Critical and culturally responsive leaders must also recognize what they need to learn and unlearn and engage in critical inquiry (Cochran-Smith, 2003a). As school leaders in diverse contexts work to challenge all forms of oppression and discrimination, they must engage in inquiry that examines how issues such as racism and diversity are understood, discussed, constructed and deconstructed. This involves learning as well as unlearning. We know from research and experience that issues such as racism and the impact on students of color are difficult to talk about in schools, not because racism does not exitst, but many White people refuse to acknowledge its presence as they fear being implicated. As Cochran-Smith points out in her work with teacher educators, as we journey there will be changes over time in terms of understanding and knowledge, language and style that we must acknowledge:

> ...to study issues of diversity and racism in teacher education, and to do so with some degree of integrity and honesty I found that I was forced to alter my perspectives as a researcher and move progressively toward a more insider, less distanced role...In doing so I began to deal with issues that blurred the boundaries of the professional and the personal...over time I not only learned about how my students constructed the issues, but I also exposed the limits of my competence, the extent of my uncertainty, and the arrogance of some of my assumptions (pp. 11–12).

To alter the educational system that is dysfunctional for particular groups of students based on race, culture, and/or language background, we need teachers [and educational leaders] who regard teaching and [leadership] as political activities and embrace social change as essential to their work (Cochran-Smith, 2003b) (Fig. 2.1).

The circle signals the ongoing learning and unlearning that school leaders go through, and that the process of learning and unlearning is fluid and ongoing. The journey of culturally responsive and social justice leadership starts with leaders having critical conversations, examining their beliefs, views on education, leadership philosophy and making a commitment to create change in their contexts. Sustainable change will not occur by itself

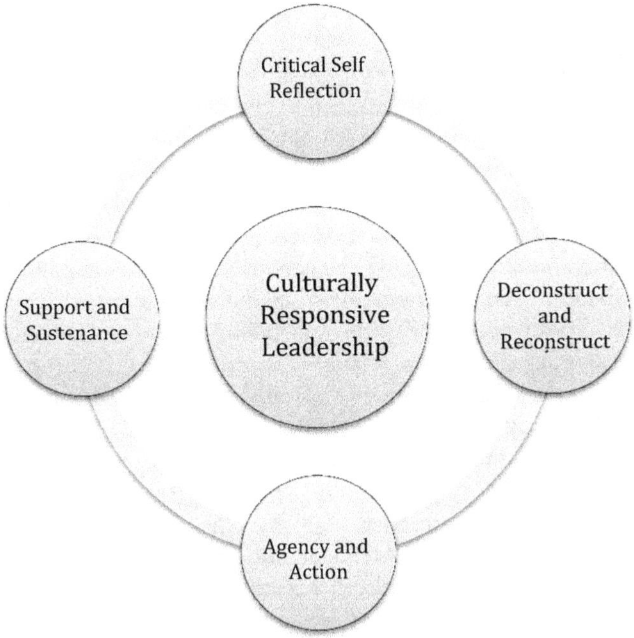

Fig. 2.1 Culturally responsive leadership model

but with commitment. Through critical reflection educational leaders examine what they bring to their role as leaders, their personal histories including their identities, values and beliefs, and how these are understood and experienced by students (Lopez, 2013). For example, school leaders who are from a higher economic status might think about how they can engage with students in their schools who might not have had similar experiences. Black school leaders in predominantly White schools might have to consider how their identity is read by their students and engage in courageous conversations about race. School leaders are encouraged to excavate hidden beliefs and assumptions that they might hold about students and teaching. Examining the inner self and our relation to the world and the community is important to how we look at educating young people (Dei, 2000).

As school leaders work to create change, they must examine current practices and seek ways to change those practices that are inequitable and construct new ways of going about schooling, re-shaping, and reconstructing processes that will benefit diverse students. This includes, for example, examining who gets sent to the office to be disciplined and suspended, the curriculum taught in the classroom, the texts that are used, the involvement of the community in decision-making in the school, the activities available to students, and so on. As school leaders begin the process of reconstructing, inclusive practices will emerge that are culturally responsive and connect to the lives and experiences of diverse students. Undergirding one's work with a level of critical consciousness guards against actions becoming opportunistic and superficial, where according to Ladson-Billings (2014) the prescribed curricula and practices go unchallenged, and where adding a few books about people of color and posting "diverse" images become accepted examples of what it means to be culturally relevant and responsive. Leaders must also be mindful of only paying lip service to issues of equity and engaging in token acts that are meaningless. The idea of developing agency is grounded in social theory and is relevant in the exercise of leadership (Frost, 2006). Durrant and Holden (2006) note that agency is the capacity to make a difference. As we work to engender change in the lives of diverse students, and indeed all students, developing agency means carving out opportunities within our educational contexts to act in collaboration with others or even sometimes alone. Critical educational theory describes empowerment as the ability to think and act critically (Giroux, 1992) and to be agentive. Agentive leaders act on behalf of those who have been marginalized, recognize that there will be tensions along the way and seek out possibilities for action. This is also a form of critical leadership that supports democracy and is action-oriented (Foster, 1989). Our identities are forged through the interpersonal connections that make up the communities that we inhabit, be that in school or out of school. Agency is also about building community with others. According to Foster (1989) schools lay the foundation for change in society, as they are learning communities in which all members have influence over themselves and others.

The road for social justice and culturally responsive leaders can be a difficult journey both professionally and personally. Oppressed people have had to fight to end segregation, to gain voting rights, to obtain womens' rights to vote and equity in the workplace. We have also had to fight for same sex couples to be married, inclusive education for those who are differently abled, Aboriginal knowledge and ways of knowing to be acknowledged, included and valued in the curriculum. We continue to fight for Black and Brown people to exercise their right to walk or drive on the streets without fear of being searched or harassed, and for justice in the courts. Schools are no different - they are a microcosm of society and reflect similar challenges. While we are aware that change can be slow and grinding we cannot give up. Educational leaders, teachers, and all progressive and critical educators need support on this journey that is tension filled (Lopez, 2005). It means developing and building a mass of critical friends and allies within the school and the community, creating safe spaces for dialogue, and finding support and mentoring that is collaborative (Lopez, 2005, 2013). In Chap. 5 I develop further the notion of collaborative mentorship (Lopez, 2005, 2013) as a means of support and sustenance for those engaged on this journey and critical path.

Social Justice Leadership

In this book I advocate for educational leadership that is culturally responsive and socially just. Above I articulate a model of culturally responsive leadership. Here I will outline briefly some of the notions of social justice leadership that higlight key conceptualizations. The purpose of social justice education is to ensure that students regardless of race, creed, color, or socio-economic status and other forms of diversity have access to and receive a good education (Cochran-Smith & Lytle, 2009). What social justice leadership is about continues to be examined; however, many educational leadership scholars and practitioners including myself have posited examples of how social justice leadership might be operationalized in different settings and contexts. Publications on social justice leadership bring to the fore examples of the work of teachers, school administrators, policy makers and others engaging in social justice work (Bogotch & Shields, 2014; Murakami-Ramalho & Pankake, 2012; Normore, 2008), to name a few. Social justice leadership, like culturally responsive leadership, can take many forms; it is not a prescription. Brooks (2012) argues that social justice "to some it is a way of looking at the world through a critical lens that highlights justice and injustice. To others it is a way of thinking about and practicing education and schooling that demands action that speaks the truth to power, rallies for freedom, liberates minds and bodies, wrests freedom from tyranny and emancipates thoughts and freedom" (p. xiii).

My journey on a path of social justice started in Jamaica where I was born and raised, experienced my early years of schooling and earned my undergraduate degree. I saw the legacies of slavery and the vestiges of colonialism that disenfranchised many and advantaged a few who owned the means of production. Poverty plagued a large majority of the people, and higher education was the privilege of a few until Michael Manley, former Prime Minister and social justice leader challenged many of the barriers that barred access for poor people. Prime Minister Michael Manley and his policies of democratic socialism advocated for education as right that should be available to all and created access for many to obtain higher education at the University of the West Indies. These experiences fueled my desire to become an educator and fight injustices not only in the education system, but society at large. Social justice leadership for me then is about finding the courage to challenge injustice. I believe that social justice leaders no matter where they are will find their space for agency to challenge injustice. I support the notion that social justice leadership is about advocacy and change, where educational leaders take bold action in schools, work to influence policy so that those who have been at the margins can be better served. Social justice is not static and as such its concept and understanding should be renewed constantly. McKenzie et al. (2008) suggest that there is no one meaning of social justice that can be universally applied, but argue for multiple approaches that include student academic achievement, varied measures of student learning, students as critical and activist members of society, and challenging curriculum that prepares students to engage with all members of society. Definitions of social justice cannot be separated from the practices of educational leadership (Bogotch, 2002; Theoharis, 2007). Leadership for social justice includes the facilitation of moral dialogue that strives for high academic achievement and affirming relationships with students from all backgrounds and ability levels as well as keeping one's epistemological awareness, value orientation, and practice toward social justice (Turhan, 2010). Educational leaders in countries across the globe continue to embrace social justice leadership in many forms as they seek to address current and emerging challenges in education.

Importance of Policy for School Leaders

Improving schools and taking action to create more culturally responsive and socially just education create possibilities for education leaders and policy makers. While a full discussion on policy is beyond the scope of this book, I think it is crucial to highlight how important it is for social justice and culturally responsive leaders to be engaged in policy making. Like others areas of education there is definitional variation with regards to policy. Some like Fowler (2013) suggest that it includes government expressed intentions and official enactments others like Knoepfl, Larrue Varone and Hill (2007) suggest that public policy is a series of intentional decisions or activities carried out with a view to solving a problem. Fowler (2013) defines policy as "the dynamic and value laden process through which a political system handles a public problem. It includes governments' expressed intensions and official enactments as well as its consistent patterns of activity and inactivity" (p. 5). Educational policies are influenced by the political environment, demographic trends and overall ideological slant in society. In the USA and some parts of Canada we have seen a push by certain groups to pass policies that impact what is taught in the curriculum and how it is taught. In some parts of the United States there is vigorous debate on how science should be taught in schools-creationism vs evolution work to influence public policy in their favor. Those on the Religious right Policies are mediated through the contexts in which they are implemented. School leaders and classroom teachers are on the front lines when it comes to the implementation of educational policies. They play an important role in defining, developing and implementing educational policy. Speaking from my experience as a school administrator and classroom teacher, implementing policies that do not take the diversity of students into account can be difficult for all those involved in education. Practicing and aspiring leaders should understand how educational policies are made and how they can be influenced (Fowler, 2013).

We have seen over and over again both in Canada and the USA how educational policies have impacted how students experience education. Much has been written about the No Child Left Behind (NCLB) policy that focused on standardization and funding mandates that negatively impacted students of color. NCLB has been replaced by Every Student Succeeds Act. Policy is important at all levels of society. In Canada the multiculturalism policy was adopted to among other things to:

- recognize and promote the cultural and racial diversity of Canadian society;
- ensure that all individuals receive equal treatment and equal protection under the law, while respecting and valuing divesity;
- foster the recognition and appreciation of the diverse cultures of Canadian society and promote the reflection and the evolvng expressions of those cultures;

While there is critique of Canada's multiculturalism policy that it masks robust dialogue about racism in Canada and racialized people continue to experience discrimination and unfair treatment, it serves to show how important policy can be in shaping public discourse and behavior.

Politicians and interest groups heavily influence educational policies. Oftentimes educators are disengaged until they have to implement them and realize that the policy is not in the best interests of diverse students. Policy influences budgets, resources, and how schools conduct business. Sometimes policy can hinder progress of diverse students and their interests. We have had experience of this in Ontario with the *Safe Schools Act* that brought about *zero tolerance* that disproportionately affected students of color and students with learning challenges. Demographic shifts, ideological shifts, and economic changes have influenced educational policies, the role of the school, leaders and teachers and how they do their job (Fowler, 2013). Fowler also suggests that in the USA demographics have contributed to a change in the policy environment that principals and vice principals are used to. Many school boards and school districts have adopted site-based management in schools and as a result school administrators find themselves dealing directly with state policymakers. Policy in education is inherently political and is interpreted differently by stakeholders whose opinions might change overtime. There is always tension involved in policy making, and policy implementation in education as policy impacts all aspects of a student's school life. For those involved in culturally responsive and socially just leadership the challenge is to ensure that educational policies do not further disadvantage those who have been underserved by the education system.

It is important for school leaders to understand the policy process that directly imapcts how they go about their work. Fowler describes the policy process as the "sequence of events that occurs when a political system considers different approaches to public problems, adopts one of them, tries it out, and evaluates it...the policy process is complex...involves the use of power" (p. 14). The importance of school leaders who seek to advance a critical agenda paying attention to educational policy cannot be overlooked, as sometimes well intentioned polices can perpetuate the injustices and inequities they seek to address. Policies that effectively address the needs of diverse learners must be a collaborative process that involves diverse community and foreground their interests and needs. Like Cochran-Smith (2003) I argue that educational leadership in pursuit of the kind of change that diverse students need requires action that affirms educational leaders as decision-makers and collaborators who must reclaim their roles in shaping of practice by taking a stand as both educators and activists. Educational leaders must engage in activism, understanding that it can be risky and must learn to be strategic about it (Ryan, 2015).

Think-Alouds—Questions for Reflection

1. How might you reconceptualize the notion of culturally responsive leadership?
2. What might be some challenges that you might encounter in your own school context implementing culturally responsive leadership and socially just educational practices and how might these be overcome?
3. How do you theorize and operationalize social justice leadership?
4. In what ways can culturally responsive and socially just leaders combat the impact of the neo-liberal and reform agenda in education?
5. Looking at the Culturally Responsive Leadership Model what might you add based on your own lived experiences as a school leader?

Research Activities

1. Research Conduct a review of the reform efforts of the Conservative Government of Ontario in the nineties. How would you assess the lasting impact on Ontario's education system?
2. Conduct a comprehensive research on the emergence and evolution of critical educational leadership theories. What are the areas of convergence and divergence? How might these theories inform your own leadership philosophy?

CHAPTER 3

Culturally Responsive Leadership and Student Engagement

Student engagement could be described as one of the most important aspects of education and learning, but there continues to be challenges with conceptualization and measurement (Sinatra, Heddy, & Lombardi, 2015), as well as terminology. Regardless, student engagement is an important goal for school leaders and most importantly those who are culturally responsive and believe in social justice. It is a simple yet complex construct that has been interpreted and theorized from multiple locations. Some educators use terminology such as *school engagemen*t while others suggest *student engagement* would be more appropriate. Regardless of terminology, the importance of student engagement to student success is recognized, as well as the negative effects of disengagement from the academic and social aspects of schools on students (Appleton, Christenson, & Furlong, 2008). Given the emergence of research showing that increased student engagement improves students' chances of success, the place of student engagement in education discourse has garnered the attention of policy makers and scholars. Student engagement, at all levels of the teaching and learning process has almost become a panacea in education for dealing with the challenges that students present. While there is no fixed definitional construct, the notion of engagement is appealing, and most importantly to educators, parents, and communities who feel the effects of student disengagement. Families and educators want students to be successful in school, become fully engaged, and improve their chances of succeeding in life. We know from research that some students are not engaged in the

A.E. Lopez, *Culturally Responsive and Socially Just Leadership in Diverse Contexts*, DOI 10.1057/978-1-137-53339-5_3

education system, not because they do not wish to learn, but because the education system does not reflect their experiences, knowledge, and identities. The students most likely to be disengaged are students of color, poor students, students who identify as gay, lesbian, or transgendered, students whose first language is not English, and immigrant students. Some scholars have argued that students are "pushed out" by the education system (Dei, Mazzuca, McIsaac, & Zine, 1997). According to Gay (2010a), schools need to become more interesting, engaging, and responsive to ethnically diverse students. This will not happen by chance. It requires focused and purposeful action by educational leaders, continuous reflection and examination of practices on their part that unconditionally value the students they serve (Kea, Trent, & Davis, 2002; Lopez, 2011).

As Gay (2000) points out, too many students of color are not achieving in school as well as they should, and the consequences of these disproportionally high levels of low achievement are long term and wide reaching. Gay suggests that "explicit knowledge about cultural diversity is imperative to meeting the needs of ethnically diverse students" (p. 107). In this chapter I reconceptualize student engagement within a framework of culturally responsive and socially just leadership. How student engagement is conceptualized is paramount to advancing the use of the construct and improving academic, social, and emotional learning outcomes for all students (Appleton et al., 2008). Some students are not doing well in school not because they are lazy and cannot learn, but because the system is not supportive of their learning. In Ontario between 35–45 % of Black, Hispanic, Portuguese, and Aboriginal students drop out of school before graduation (Toronto District School Board, 2010). In the USA research has shown that African American students do not have good experiences at school, and often have low expectations, a feeling of inferiority, and a sense of defeat in academic pursuits (Cooper & Jordan, 2003).

Defining Student Engagement

The concept of student engagement has evolved over the years and is still emerging. It has primarily and historically been about increasing achievement, positive behaviors, and sense of belonging in the classroom (Harris, 2008; Willms, Friesen, & Milton, 2009). In its earliest conceptions student engagement was primarily meant to re-engage predominantly socioeconomically disadvantaged students who were at risk of dropping out of high school (Taylor & Parsons, 2011). Some have argued that there is no fixed definition of student engagement, as multiple factors are at play when students are fully engaged in learning. The relevance of student engagement has been established but how it is measured and defined remains contentious. Harris (2008) review of student engagement suggests that "while there is general agreement that student engagement produces positive outcomes, defining the concept is problematic as there is disagreement about what counts as student engagement" (p. 58).

Fredericks, Blumenfeld, and Paris (2004) posit that student engagement is a multidimensional construct that offers great promise in understanding the complexities of children's experiences in school that allow us to design more nuanced and targeted interventions. They identified three key categories—behavioral, emotional, and cognitive. Other notions of student engagement have been posited that include, for example, how students are supported to achieve academically, develop positive behaviors, and acquire a sense of belonging in the classroom (Harris, 2008; Willms et al., 2009). Also included are psychological dimensions (Anderson, Christenson, Sinclair, & Lehr, 2004), intellectual capacity (Dunleavy, Milton, & Crawford, 2010) and respectful relationships between teachers and students (Covell, McNeil, & Howe, 2009). While much of the literature on student engagement focuses on behavioral, cognitive, emotional, and agentic engagement (Cleary & Zimmerman, 2012; Finn & Rock, 1997; Fredericks et al., 2004; Greene, Miller, Crowson, Duke, & Akey, 2004; Heddy & Sinatra, 2013; Linnenbrink-Garcia & Pekrun, 2011; Reeve, 2012; Reeve & Tseng, 2011), the extant literature is sparse on the impact of culturally responsive and social justice practices on student engagement, particularly for ethnically diverse, racialized, and minoritized students. McMahon and Portelli (2004) call these approaches into question as they do not challenge the underlying reasons for disengagement for some students, which include curriculum that do not reflect their experiences and pedagogy that they see as oppressive. They argue that any conversation about student engagement must include conversations of what school is about - the underlying purposes of schooling and ways that schooling practices reinforce exclusion. McMahon and Portelli (2004) examine student engagement from three perspectives and paradigms—conservative/traditional, neo-liberal, and transformative. The conservative approach theorizes student engagement through behavior traits, academic achievement, and psychological dispositions that see engagement primarily as compliance and adhering to school norms. The Neo-liberal approach values the role of the community but implicitly it is also about compliance focused on singular behavior or achievement. The transformative approach calls for student engagement from a critical-democratic perspective that challenges the status quo and practices that oppress students. Student engagement must include democratic transformation, ongoing dialogue between teachers and students, and critique of the socio-economic context of schooling and communities that they serve. They argue further that student engagement is enacted "through the interactions of students and teachers, in a shared space, for the purpose of democratic reconstruction, through which personal transformation takes place" (McMahon & Portelli, 2004, p. 70). I support this transformative approach to student engagement and it is the approach that I encourage school leaders who are culturally responsive and socially just to embrace.

Notwithstanding the definitional multiplicity of student engagement and its multidimensional nature, educators recognize the devastating effects of disengagement in school on the lives of young people and society. Appleton et al. (2008) found that students were less engaged in high school if they were male; from an ethnic group other than White or Asian; were from lower socio-economic levels; or were in special education classes. Given the impact of disengagement, particularly on ethnically diverse students, student engagement and achievement have become a focus and priority for educational leaders. Harris (2008) suggests that greater emphasis needs to be placed on the environment that is created for learning in which students feel supported and motivated, see purpose, engage in critical thinking, and feel committed. If students are to have meaningful relationships in school they need to see fairness and have trust (Dunleavy & Milton, 2009). Students must feel safe to engage in dialogue and challenge knowledge that is presented (Taylor & Parsons, 2011).

In Canada student engagement is considered an important issue at all levels (provincial, district, and school) to address dropout rates, foster active citizenship, and improve achievement (Dunleavy, 2009). How student engagement is conceptualized and the theoretical framework foregrounded matters (Appleton et al., 2008). What is meant by engagement varies with both the theoretical perspective of the researcher and the level at which engagement is conceptualized, observed, and measured, which could range from the individual to the community (Sinatra et al., 2015). Sinatra et al., refer to this way of looking at the issue of engagement as "grain size", and suggest that the theoretical orientation of the researcher might impact the conclusions drawn. As such researchers should make their "grain size" clear when theorizing about student engagement.

I suggest that student engagement is also an issue of equity and social justice that impacts diverse students and their experiences in the teaching and learning process. The question of engagement for students of color and racial minority students stretches across the K-20 spectrum. College students, like students in K-12, have called for more culturally responsive curricula and suggest there is a disregard for multiculturalism, with limited opportunities to learn about their cultural selves and diverse others in the classroom (Quaye & Harper, 2007). Students perceive education as disconnected from their experiences when it does not acknowledge, respect, and connect to their experiences and perspectives and hostile learning environments create marginalization of some students and interfere with their learning (Baxter, 2001). I agree with (McMahon, Munns, Smyth & Zyngier, 2012) when they assert that student engagement "should respect and incorporate the identities, cultures, and lives of the students; involving students in decision-making about topics, protocols, and activities; and enacting curricula that are authentic, meaningful, and challenging" (p. 74) and this must be part of a social justice agenda.

Reconceptualizing Student Engagement in a Culturally Responsive and Socially Just Framework

Culturally responsive educational leaders have a responsibility to seek out change in the school environment and positively impact the experiences of students. The theoretical grounding for my conceptualization of student engagement is based on Freire's notion of school as a space for challenging oppression. Reconceptualizing student engagement as a way of disrupting deficit approaches to ethnically diverse and poor students where their experiences, knowledge, and cultural ways of being are seen as deficiencies to overcome is important for critical educators. Zyngier (2008) suggests that student engagement must achieve social justice and academic achievement simultaneously and must take into account the socio-economic and cultural backgrounds of students. In doing so, student engagement can no longer be seen in terms of behavior of the student, but as part of a larger system of oppression. Schlossberg (1989) suggests that when students feel marginalized they feel as if they do not fit in and this can lead to negative outcomes such as depression and poor behavior. It is important to create culturally relevant experiences in higher education as well to support ethnically diverse and low-income students where the issue of student engagement still persists for these students (Kezar, Walpole, & Perna, 2014). From the research it has become clear that students are placed at risk when the learning environment does not respond to their needs (Reschly & Christenson, 2012). Diverse students continue to face a different set of challenges in schools and colleges (Quaye & Harper, 2015) that impede their success.

Educational leadership scholars and researchers who work and research within social justice and culturally responsive frameworks (Beachum, 2011; Bogotch, 2005; Brooks, Normore, & Jean-Marie, 2014; Furman, 2012; Ryan, 2014; Shields, 2010) have examined ways to address improved learning outcomes for diverse students. Many scholars have argued that disengagement from the schooling process by students of color has fed the *school-to-prison pipeline*, as students who do not succeed in school are by far the largest percentage of those in jails. Appleton et al. (2008) suggest that "students at high risk for school failure based on status variables such as ethnicity, home language, race, and/or socio-economic level can be differentiated by their amount of participation in and/or identification with the tasks and activities of the school, and these differences are related to important outcomes such as academic achievement and persistence with academic work" (p. 374). It is difficult for diverse students to be engaged with the tasks and activities of the school when those tasks and activities do not reflect their interests. It is clear that student engagement must be thought about differently and school leaders have a role to play. Dantley and Tillman (2010) argue that leadership must be socially just and by doing so investigate the challenges that we face in schools today and offer solutions. Ryan (2006) suggests "inclusive leadership consists of a number of distinct practices that include advocating for inclusion, educating participants, developing critical consciousness, nurturing dialogue, emphasizing student learning and classroom practice, adopting inclusive decision and policymaking strategies, and incorporating whole school approaches" (p. 9). Ogbu (2003) and others have conducted studies that show that higher engagement is associated with lower dropout rates. When success is not achieved poor performance ensues and students drop out (Finn, 1989). The education system has been inconsistent in educating students across racial and ethnic groups, and these students are more often than not disengaged from school.

Bingham and Okagaki (2012) suggest that ethnicity and other factors of identity should factor in the discourse on student engagement given the demographic shifts taking place in schools. Demographic shifts create an imperative for school leaders to improve the educational outcomes for this new diverse majority that will require more supports to be successful in education systems that do not necessarily represent their experiences (Maxwell, 2014). The underachievement of African American, Latino/a, and American Indian (Aboriginal) children in the USA (and Canada) has in part been attributed to the lack of engagement in school (Steele, 1997). Social anthropologist Ladson-Billings (2014) argues when the cultural practices of students are devalued in schools they may experience failure. When students perceive that there is discrimination or they experience discrimination this affects their engagement and achievement in school (Bingham & Okagaki, 2012). Similarly, when racial and ethnic minority students believe that they are doing well in school this has an impact on their lives and contributes to their engagement and achievement in school (Sue & Okazaki, 1990).

In the model below I reconceptualize student engagement within a framework of culturally responsive and socially just theory and practices, drawing on the findings of my research with school leaders and teacher leaders, and drawing on the literature and scholarly work in the field (Appleton et al., 2008; Eccles, Wigfield, & Schiefle, 1998; Finn, 1989; Fredericks et al., 2004; Fredricks & McColskey, 2012; McMahon & Portelli, 2004; McMahon, Munns, Smyth & Zyngier, 2012). I believe the experiences of culturally responsive and socially just school leaders and teachers are important to how we understand and conceptualize student engagement. I envision student engagement as a process that occurs over the course of a student's life in school from K- 20. This re-thinking was spurred when one of my graduate students, an instructor at the college level in Ontario, Canada, said she was taking the class that I was teaching called *Student Success, Student Engagement and Diversity* because she wanted to learn from the K-12 setting ways to engage students in the college where she works and higher education in general. She suggested that while engagement was an issue overall in colleges, she noticed that ethnically diverse students and students from low-income groups were adversely impacted by lack of engagement as there seems to be a greater focus on student engagment at the K-12 level.

We know from research that some students are disengaged before they get to high school, and on the other end of the spectrum many have argued that more needs to be done in higher education to meet the needs of ethnically diverse students (see Quaye & Harper, 2015). The behavioral, emotional, and cognitive (Appleton et al., 2008; Fredericks et al., 2004) aspects of student engagement speak to the needs of students in developing positive relationships, managing conflict well, having a good sense of self, and excelling in the cognitive domains by doing well in their academic work. The other aspects of the model speak to issues that are important to culturally responsive and socially just school leaders who take a critical approach to schooling, argue for the removal of school structures and practices that oppress some students, and also challenge deficit approaches to teaching and learning. The status quo that reinforces dominant ideology does not work for some students. Their cultural background and experiences must be included and the knowledge that resides in communities must be brought to bear on the teaching and learning context. Learning occurs when organizations adapt to changing environments, learn from the past, and engage in continuous innovation (Arygis & Schon, 1996). Ethnically diverse students and students from low-income communities do not want to be spoken about all the time in terms of deficits and be constantly labeled "at-risk", "hard to serve", "challenging" and "disadvantaged". Harper and Quaye (2015) call on educators to be strategic and intentional about fostering conditions that compel students to make the most of college, both inside and outside the classroom, as dependency is no longer applicable given the increased diversity of students. At the college level Harper (2013) suggests that more attention needs to be paid to the environment in which men of color, Black men, Latino men, and all minoritized and racialized students learn. In writing about minoritized and racialized students Harper (2013) notes:

> They are outnumbered ... their grade point averages are among the lowest of all undergraduate students, their engagement in classrooms and enriching out-of-class experiences is alarming low, and their attrition rates are comparatively higher than those of White students in the U.S higher education... Encounters with racism, racial stereotypes, microaggressions, and low expectations from professors and others undermine their academic outcomes, sense of belonging, and willingness to seek help and utilize campus resources (p. 3).

Many would argue that this is the experience of minoritized and racialized students in elementary and secondary schools in most Western countries. The issue of engagement and disengagement cannot be placed solely on students' attitudes and behaviors, and not on the schooling contexts. The onus of engagement on students alone is misplaced (Harper, Berhanu, Davis, & McGuire, 2015; Kimbrough & Harper, 2006). Zyngier (2008) argues that student engagement requires engaged pedagogy that highlights the following principles:

- Connects to and engages with the cultural knowledge of students.
- Students are represented in the curriculum, see themselves in their work, and own the process of teaching and learning.
- Teachers respond to and include the lived experiences of students and empower them to actively and consciously critique their experiences.
- Students are empowered by the teaching and learning process and their experiences at school that allow them to live their lives in ways that make them feel fulfilled and provide space for their voice in the school environment.

School leaders and teachers in the studies understood student engagement in terms of academic success, feeling valued and respected in the school environment, participation in school activities, and improved behavior. Participants were asked the following question: How would you describe the effectiveness of culturally responsive leadership practices in your school and its impact on student engagement and achievement? They felt student engagement was a key outcome of their efforts as culturally responsive leaders. They described student engagement in terms of improvements in grades, increased excitement and interest in learning, greater involvement of parents, and less disciplinary issues. The participants were mindful of not resorting to control and compliance (Zyngier, 2008) but rather respectful engagement with students. This is in keeping with (McMahon, Munns, Smyth & Zyngier, 2012) who found that students want to be treated with respect, feel included and have a curricula that is engaging and authentic. This can be a tricky road to travel for culturally responsive and socially just leaders who believe in schooling that empowers students but sometimes conflict with existing school rules and processes that do not take into account the experiences of diverse students–rules and processes that many students will tell you they feel oppressed by. As an administrator I recall many instances where the "no hat" policy in the school created conflict between teachers and students and led to the suspension of some students who felt that they were being unfairly targeted. One vice principal with over twenty years of experience who worked in a very diverse elementary school with a large population of predominantly Black and South Asian students noted that "the students became energized particularly around school activities showcasing their culture" and the teachers at her school said there were less discipline issues, and greater interest in reading as the books used in literature circles reflected the culture and experiences of the students". Another principal with seventeen years of experience noted that she used culturally responsive practices to "keep students in school and prevent them from dropping out". These included supporting teachers to be culturally responsive in their teaching and pedagogy, allocating funds to purchase resources, actively involving the community in the life of the school, being visible to the students, listening to their concerns, and responding in genuine ways. She also noted that she has seen that "students are more inclined to be involved with their learning if they see themselves in the curriculum that is connected to their experiences". One school leader who worked in both elementary and secondary schools said that it was important for her "to make connections between home and school experiences" and she saw the "improvement in behaviour that this made". The teachers noted improved levels of performance in both oral and written assessments, behavior, and interest in the subject and content when culturally responsive texts and instructional approaches were used in Grade 9 and Grade 12 English classrooms (see Lopez, 2011, 2014). One teacher leader noted "that there was increased participation, improvement in grades, and enhanced critical thinking skills, and most importantly, students became active participants in their own learning".

The school leaders in the research found that students were far more engaged (had more interest in their academic work, participated more in school activities, got better grades, had improvement in literacy skills) "when the school actively involved the parents and the community". Another principal noted there was "a marked improvement in reading when she started a book club that included parents and the community". Increased family involvement was a consistent theme throughout, from the school leaders. Gonzalez, Moll, and Amanti (2005) in *Funds of Knowledge* suggest that when the culture of the home is brought into the classroom it is a richer learning experience for students.

> As discourses come to recognize that situated nature of knowledge and the partiality of all knowledge claims, the metaphor of border-crossers has been foregrounded. However, the ultimate border-the border between knowledge and power –can be crossed only when educational institutions no longer reify culture, when lived experiences become validated as a source of knowledge, and when the process of how knowledge is constructed and translated between groups located within nonsymmmetrical relations of power is questioned. (Gonzalez et al., 2005, p. 42).

One principal in a grade 7 school reported that she saw a "marked improvement in behaviour and attendance" when she became "more intentional in involving the community in planning activities in the school". She also indicated that she tried "to get to know the students" as in her words "she wanted them to feel safe and connected to the school". Many of the school leaders in the study talked about how important it was to adopt a caring approach and model when dealing with students. One participant wrote that "some teachers complain that minoritized students are not engaged, but they really do not get to know them". Research continually points to the importance of getting to know students and connececting with them on various levels. When academic knowledge and skills are situated within the lived experiences of students, they are more personally meaningful, learned more easily and thoroughly (Gay, 2000). Paris (2012) calls for culturally sustaining pedagogy that seeks to perpetuate and foster linguistic, literate, and cultural pluralism as part of the democratic project of schooling. Community engagement speaks to the knowledge that resides in the homes and communities of diverse learners that is important in supporting their engagement with school (Fig. 3.1).

My work with school administrators and teacher leaders confirms that it is important for educators to go beyond their comfort zone and learn about other cultures in non-stereotypical ways in order to engage students. Student engagement increases when students see themselves in the curriculum through texts and other activities (Lopez, 2011). At the K-12 level and in higher education, research has made the connection between engagement and achievement—those who become disengaged, or are not engaged, and those who underachieve tend to be students from marginalized populations. It is not only important to pay attention to issues of

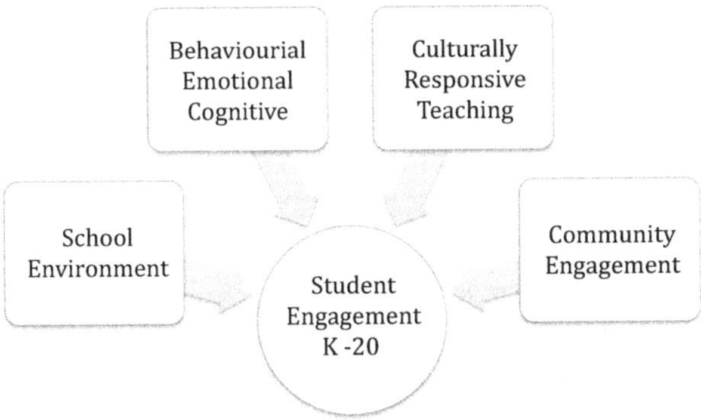

Fig. 3.1 Conceptual model of student engagement and culturally responsive leadership

diversity in K-12 schools, but in higher education as well. Embracing a culturally responsive and socially just approach is an effective tool for student engagement, improved learning outcomes, democracy outcomes—more engaged citizenry, promotes active thinking, and developmental goals. Student engagement is not standard or monolithic. Many have argued that there needs to be variety in approach as educators seek to put in place strategies to support diverse students. Education for humanization involves engaging students in ways that affirm them and their role in the world. This involves ensuring that students have voice, that educational leaders continue to examine their practices, challenge assumptions and biases, and create new epistemologies on which they can ground their actions. This critical self-reflection is important for educational leaders to engage in transformative work (Shields, 2010) and is important for culturally responsive and socially just leaders. Khalifa, Gooden, and Davis (2016) argue that critical reflection must form the foundation of the work culturally responsive leaders do who are seeking to create meaningful change on behalf of students.

Think Alouds—Questions for Reflection

1. How would you reconceptualize student engagement within the context of diversity?
2. What factors support student engagement in your school?
3. What would you add to the model of student engagement posited based on your own experience?
4. What might those in higher education learn from student engagement efforts in K-12 schools?

Research Activity

1. Examine the evolution of the literature on student engagement. Create a visual to show the evolution of the concept. How might scholars and researchers begin to think about student engagement differently within the context of increasing diversity in schools?
2. Review and examine the effectiveness of student engagement policies on lowering the drop-out rate in your school board or local district? How might a culturally responsive approach support those efforts?

CHAPTER 4

Tensions of Practice

The work of critical educators is not easy and can be tension filled. The idea of highlighting the tensions that school leaders face come from research that I previously conducted with classroom teachers (Lopez, 2005). I worked with classroom teachers who wanted to be proactive in changing their curriculum to be more reflective of the diversity they were seeing in their classrooms, and needed a space to be open and vulnerable about issues that were creating tensions for them. Teachers in the study engaged in research to critically examine their journey as teachers to be more inclusive in their practices and deal with challenges and dissonance that they experienced. The findings of that research highlighted the importance of acknowledging and recognizing tensions that practitioners face on their journey to be culturally responsive and socially just, and to use these tensions as moments of learning. Focusing on tensions that school leaders experience allows us to capture the feelings of internal turmoil that educators experience as they encounter different competing demands (Berry, 2008).

Tensions and conflicts are part of the everydayness of school leadership that includes dilemmas, paradoxes, and contradictions that have been ignored (Bogotch & Reyes-Guerra, 2014). The demographic shifts that have taken place in society and schools have impacted how school leaders operate and the expectations placed on them to react to this change to meet the needs of the growing diversity of students. The pace and complexity of this shift have caused tensions to surface for school leaders, teachers, parents, and communities. The school is often the only space where people

A.E. Lopez, *Culturally Responsive and Socially Just Leadership in Diverse Contexts*, DOI 10.1057/978-1-137-53339-5_4

from different racial, ethnic, national, and religious backgrounds spend considerable time together (Wessler, 2011) and as such must seek ways to build community from difference. Schools help people make sense of the changes that are taking place in society, as well as foster lifelong learning. Society's most important investment is increasingly seen to be education of its people. We suffer in the absence of good education and prosper in its presence (Mulford, 2003b). I argue that good education involves dealing with diversity in positive ways that empower students and their communities. Increasing diversity in schools has caused educators to think about what it means to lead, as schools and those who lead them are important to the success of students (Mulford, 2003a).

This chapter looks at the tensions that culturally responsive and socially just leaders face within the context of growing diversity. Researchers and scholars have examined the challenges that school leaders must deal with in an era of school reform and school improvement mandates focused primarily on testing and one-size-fits-all approaches to school improvement. School leaders who engage in culturally responsive and socially just approaches face unique challenges in addition to the regular day-to-day challenges found in schools. Some have argued that the breath of challenges that school leaders face have caused the role of the school leader at the principal level to become less attractive. According to Mulford (2003b) there is a shortage of school leaders, primarily principals because of the view that the role is too challenging and there is not enough support in the face of increasing demands.

Some of the earlier studies on the challenges that school leaders face focused on tensions in managing change (Day, Harris, & Hadfield, 2001), functions of the role and pressures of adjusting to constantly changing reform and improvement agenda (Edmunds, Mulford, Kendall, & Kendall, 2008). Castle and Mitchell (2001) in their research conducted with elementary school principals in Canada found that managing competing goals created tensions for school leaders. These competing goals included the volume of managerial demands that took time away from their role as instructional leaders, balancing their responsibility of supporting teachers and students with the authority aspects of the role, implementing change at a pace that did not create instability, and relationship building with others versus focusing on control of personal work environment. Edmunds et al. (2008) suggest that principals experience a leadership dilemma when they can no longer deconstruct the purposes of imposed changes in the system that they sometimes see as incongruent with the needs of their students. Other tensions and dilemmas that principals experience and manage as part of their work include issues such as performance on professional tasks, their personal versus institutional imperatives, leadership in small schools versus large schools, and managing responses to demands from outside the school.

Increased diversity in schools has caused the role of the leader to become illuminated as the nature and scope of the work changes. In the post-industrial era where society has changed significantly this has affected the role of the educational leader, which has been further impacted by advances in technology and the flow of information as more continues to be expected of them (OEDC, 2001). Tyack and Cuban (1995) warned that those responsible for schools must be careful, because education can easily shift from being seen as a panacea for solving problems to being made into the scapegoat for all the many ills of society. The competing interests and ideas that permeate the discourse about society in Canada, the USA, and many Western countries have impacted the discourse on the role of education in society and hence the role of schools. Understanding the conflicts and tensions that practitioners face is crucial to practitioners', reformers', and researchers' understanding of how these communities cope and are sustained over time (Achinstein, 2002). Achinstein suggests that understanding tensions and conflicts within a community creates contexts for learning and ongoing renewal. If change is to be made in how educational leaders do their work, tensions that occur on the job cannot be ignored.

School leaders in the study shared examples of feeling overwhelmed keeping up with the daily demands of their role, the impact of the changes in technology on how they do their jobs, demands to create school improvement plans that are reflective of the students the school serves dealing without adequate resources, resistance from colleagues and members of the community who sometimes have different expectations of what inclusion and equity means and looks like, and keeping up with their own professional learning. They found it challenging managing all these demands and responsibilities all at the same time. Blackmore (2009) suggests that there is reluctance to address the structural and cultural factors that are important in practice. "Nothing is ever easy". one teacher leader remarked:

> ...If you want to start a club you need others to assist you because you cannot do everything by yourself...you don't have enough time and it gets overwhelming...you have to build relationships with people and explain what you are about and why you are doing things that way...and sometimes

> you face resistance because people don't see the need for change…sometimes it is from other colleagues, sometimes it is from members of the community who are also resistant to change (Valerie, teacher leader).

Berry (2008) in her research with pre-service teachers that examined the tensions that they experienced highlighted the following areas that were of concern to them: (1) telling and growth—what she describes as finding the space and courage to create new opportunities for growth; (2) confidence and uncertainty dealing with and making explicit the complexities of teaching; (3) finding the courage to take action and be purposeful; (4) the need for safety and a safe space to discuss issues with others; (5) the need to be responsive to the realities in one's context, setting up contexts for learning and recognizing possibilities within them; (6) valuing and reconstructing experience based on new knowledge and insights that emerge. There are convergences in my research with Berry, particularly around the need for space to discuss issues that are troubling where those issues can be discussed and deconstructed. There are convergences as well on the need to take action that is purposful and challenges current norms.

Davis (2002) argues that the efforts of culturally responsive leaders are often met with many obstacles or "walls" as she describes them. These "walls" take many different forms and can emerge from policies, teachers, students, colleagues and communities. The school leaders in the study expressed "feeling perplexed" at times. This included balancing their individual philosophy, ideology, lived experiences, with actions that they were sometimes asked to take that created conflicts in the contexts in which they worked. Culturally responsive and social justice leaders seek to break away from the more functional models of leadership that have been in schools for many years, that sometimes place too much emphasis efficiency and resource management. Culturally responsive leaders seek to focus on building relationships with students and communities. A principal in an elementary school wrote that she was often frustrated when some teachers did not see the need and urgency to make their teaching and curriculum more culturally responsive and relevant:

> I get frustrated when some teachers do not see why it is important for their teaching and resources used in their classrooms to be culturally relevant and responsive. I work with my teachers and support them. This takes time. I just cannot tell them this is how it is going to happen and expect them to just take my word for it. The teachers need time to reflect and come to their own understanding (Jane, principal).

Tensions that school leaders in the study shared were both personal and professional. When we are challenged and conflicted we are impacted both personally and professionally as we bring ourselves to our various roles as educators. The self is always implicated in how we understand and carry out our roles in schools. In this regard I draw on micropolitical theories and perspectives (Achinstein, 2002; Ball, 1987; Blase, 1991b) to help unpack the tensions that arose for school leaders in the study. Micropolitical theories spotlight individual differences, diversity of objectives, conflict, uses of informal power, the negotiated and interpretive nature of organizations, offer a lens for understanding and uncovering power, influence, conflict, as well as negotiating processes between individuals and groups within school organizations (Achinstein, 2000). Micropolitical theories help us to think about the day-to-day actions that are necessary in any organization to help us survive and navigate situations that are difficult. School leaders in the study engaged in various micropolitical activities such as finding allies to work with, collaborating on issues with colleagues who did not necessarily think about schooling the way they did, learning how to build relationships across interests, learning when to forge ahead on an issue and when to say that can wait for another time, becoming astute at understating their context and the people they work with, negotiating, and learning not to take resistance personally.

Micropolitical theory helps us to understand what goes on in organizations at the local level, as well as the level of the individual (Ball, 1987). Armstrong, Tuters, and Carrier (2013) in their research with school leaders in Ontario found that school leaders who wanted to enact social justice leadership and attempted to translate equity policies into practice were often met with micropolitical tactics in the form of overt and/or covert resistance to their efforts. Education is a political endeavor (Giroux, 1992) as each stakeholder group involved (students, teachers, parents, school leaders, bureaucrats, policy makers) engage from varying ideological perspectives and according to what they believe the purpose of education should be in society. This reality adds to the complexity of education and schooling, where competing ideas play out and tensions arise. There are varying ideas about education, and these issues play out not only in the public discourse, but schooling practices each day. These issues range from who sits on the school council to how different cultures are represented in school activities.

Schools are complex political arenas where divergent purposes and values often compete and coexist (Blase, 1993). Bjork and Blaise (2009) argue that political activity involves conflicting as well as cooperative processes where stakeholders wrestle with their values, ideologies, interactions with others, and balancing interests. I theorize the tensions that school leaders shared in what I call *tensions of practice*. These *tensions of practice* help to develop understanding and foster learning among school leaders as they navigate and traverse their journey. Ryan (2012) suggests that principals engage in a variety of activities such as developing alliances and relationships, persuading others to join their cause, acting reflectively and consciously, using rewards to create alliances, modeling, providing different kinds of support to colleagues, and being visible as they engage in micropolitical activities to navigate their contexts. Armstrong et al. (2013) argue that "social justice leadership is moral and political work, and a micropolitical lens helps to illuminate the boundaries of politics and power as they intersect with equity beliefs and behaviours in schools" (p. 123).

Tensions of Practice

The journey of culturally responsive and socially just leaders is not an easy one with cleary defined outcomes. It is a journey filled wirh complexities that are impacted by the contexts in which leaders find themselves. It is a lifelong journey and a struggle that will carry on well beyond our lifetime. Social justice and culturally responsive leaders are, however, buoyed by the knowledge that their efforts benefit students, and in particular diverse students. As one school leader remarked, "engaging in culturally responsive and social justice leadership is a journey not a straight line. It is a journey of many critical incidents or moments that inform my understanding". Critical incidents are moments that cause reflection and deep learning for educators in their professional contexts and lives. I use an analogy from my days as an Economics teacher in secondary school; That is, the long-run position is made of a series of short-run positions. In much the same way, the journey of educational leaders on a path to creating lasting and sustainable change over time will be comprised of many small actions. While the participants revealed many moments that were tension-filled for them, I highlight the following areas that were consistent among participants: (1) Resistance from colleagues, (2) Addressing the needs of the community, (3) Balancing personal and professional lives,

(4) Building capacity and ongoing learning, and (5) Dealing with the challenges of racism.

Resistance from Colleagues

As culturally responsive and socially just leaders we must expect resistance to our work as we challenge the status quo and push for change. A number of the participants talked about combating a vision of leadership among colleagues (principals and teachers) that was "not ready to embrace change in critical ways that pushed boundaries". A wilingness simply to go along with the status quo. One principal remarked, "some colleagues do not have the willingness to support change and it becomes even more challenging when that position is held by senior leadership". This principal felt that it was sometimes not prudent to "go against senior leadership" particularly if your are the only one. Another reminded me of the old saying in schools "don't let that be a career-limiting move". Sometimes this dissonance was not only ideological, but also reflected in how resources were allocated for various activities. One participant noted that at times "it felt like the leaders above her wanted to play it safe and not offend anyone or create conflict". A teacher leader was conflicted about the "pace of change when it comes to diverse students" and the "extra caution" that she noted particularly around the hiring of diverse staff.

Another area of tension was in the understanding of what culturally responsive and social justice leadership looks like in the classroom and the school. A principal with over twenty years of experience who spent her life advocating for a more culturally responsive curricula that reflect the experiences of the students in schools felt that she was "constantly battling the celebratory notion of equity and social justice" where, as she puts it, "it is easy to add samosas to the cuisine in the cafeteria but there is a reluctance to look at the Math or the History curriculum and create deep lasting change in instruction and materials". It is "hard work to convince colleagues it is the right thing to do…it takes building relationships and finding allies, and not giving up". It is important for educators to find ways of dealing with resistance effectively so that it does not eat away at your passion and desire for change. Some argue that peace education is an effective way of dealing with resistance (See Bajaj, 2015). Bajaj suggests that educational spaces can be sites of possibility and transformation, but critical educators must learn strategies for peace, and pay attention to the format, structure, and methods in order to promote good intentions among others.

Addressing the Needs of the Community

Being culturally responsive and socially just means ensuring that diverse communities are involved and reflected in the life of the school, and that they are involved in decision-making that will impact their children. With the demographic shifts experienced in Ontario communities and schools have changed. This change has caused tensions for some school leaders as they have to respond to the needs of communities differently, often in ways that some are not used to doing. School leaders in this context must react to cultural and other forms of diversity as they address the needs of students and communities. The new reality calls for school leaders and most importantly school administrators to get to to know the customs and traditions of the people in the communities that they serve. The tensions expressed by participants were twofold: (1) the need to connect with new and emerging communities; and (2) educating parents who expressed stereotypical and prejudicial views in response to demographic shifts. One principal noted that sometimes she felt like she was walking a tightrope in conversations with parents:

> I sometimes feel like I am walking a tight rope when I engage with parents. I have to spend time explaining to some parents the reasons why some actions are taken and necessary to support students and not giving favors (Jennifer, principal).

Some participants expressed tensions not getting to know the communities fast enough as they would have liked and the ongoing work that is required to understand the uniqueness of each community. This is similar to Armstrong et al.'s (2013) findings where school leaders indicated "achieving consensus around common social justice goals was difficult because of conflicting interests and values and people's inability to see beyond narrow personal and political agendas" (p. 126). Community involvement at all levels is important in a social justice agenda. Educational leaders cannot be tourists in the communities that they serve and work. This is even more important in diverse communities where more often than not, the school administrator is not from that community or reflects the diversity ethnically, culturally or racially. Research shows that that the majority of school administrators remain predominantly White as the school population becomes more diverse, particularly diverse communities. Diverse communites need school leaders who are attentive to their needs.

Balancing Personal and Professional Lives

The school leaders talked about tensions balancing their personal and professional lives and feeling "burnt out" at times. Creating lasting change in schools does not happen overnight. It requires investment of time and emotion. Even without taking on this additional work and responsibility some teachers and school leaders complain of burn out from the share volume of work. Work-life balance is important for an individual's psychological well-being, self-esteem, satisfaction, and overall sense of harmony in life. Balancing these aspects in one's life can be regarded as indicators of a successful balance between work and family roles (Clark, Koch, & Hill, 2004). School leaders, particularly principals and vice principals, found that the pace and busyness of schools meant that there was not always time "to make that extra phone call to a parent or take on supervising an activity" that was important. One elementary principal noted:

> I have been at this for a long time. I worked on equity issues before I came to this board. I worked in one of the neighborhoods of Toronto that everyone likes to stereotype. Yes, they have challenges there of high poverty and the need is great...but you cannot ignore the work that needs to be done (Adele, principal).

Maintaining work—life balance as an educator involves continuous reflection and making intentional choices—a process that occurs over time. It is important, to prevent burnout, that school leaders work toward a healthy work—life balance. Trying to maintain this balance is an ongoing issue for many educators. Challenges maintaining a healthy work work life balance has been noted among teachers who work in urban areas who reported feeling professional isolation and feeling unprepared to teach in diverse schools (Darling-Hammond, 2003). Durham-Barnes (2011) suggests that issues of isolation and unpreparedness create tensions in the personal lives of teachers and ways should be found to sustain and support them in these times of struggle and tension. I believe that this also applies to school leaders and was evident from the research. Grossman (1995) notes that tension in diverse communities sometimes come from cultural disconnect between teachers and their students. And I would add between school leaders and the communities they serve. Working with teachers and school leaders who are from the dominant group to effectively navigate diverse communities will will go along way in easing ease some of the tensions they experience.

Building Capacity and Ongoing Learning

The school leaders in the study felt that it was important for them to have had professional development to support the culturally responsive work that they were doing. One principal noted, "there are professional development workshops in my board that I attend. These are mainly stand alone. What I need is ongoing professional development on culturally responsive leadership and how I can implement it better in my school and support my teachers". Another principal at a secondary school talked about his own development as a culturally responsive leader after he "examined his thinking and practices around the unevenness of suspensions that students of color received in his school" and the impact that had on him and his won journey. He "vowed to do something about it". Critical scholars have highlighted the experiential nature of engaging culturally responsive and social justice work that emerges from practice in very organic ways and changes our conceptualization of how we should be as educators. These experiences help us to move beyond theorizing, and find examples of what is possible from our own experiences in schools. These examples are important so that others can learn from them.

Building capacity among educational leaders is important if change is to occur (Fullan, 2005a). Panakake and Abrego (2012) suggest that "building capacity requires opportunities for educators to engage in identifying their shared beliefs and values, to examine ways in which personal and professional values and beliefs align with those of others and, most importantly, with the principles social justice demands" (p. 7). Educational leaders must be prepared to understand how their work, advocacy, and agenda for social justice education are important aspects of their professional capital (Murakami-Ramalho & Panakake, 2012). Forde (2014) argues that "theorization must be accompanied by critique which is imbued by ideas of social justice [diversity and difference], fairness and equality [equity] (p. 140)". School leaders promote culturally responsive teaching by demonstrating culturally responsive approaches themselves as leaders, in their relations with parents, teachers, and students. This means developing agency on behalf of disadvantaged students, engaging in purposeful complex actions that build relationships with different stakeholders, understanding the complexity of schools, and finding spaces to do the work that needs to be done (Riehl, 2000). If the work of school leaders is to improve then it is important that these capacities be fully embedded in principal preparation programs, and ongoing professional development that school leaders receive. This will not happen by chance. School leaders must become actively engaged in finding new ways to go about the business of schooling—that will ensure the full involvement of all students and communities.

Dealing with Racism

School leaders in the study noted that there were tensions discussing issues of race and racism in the school system. One participant noted that it "felt like a taboo to talk about how race impacted some students, particularly Black boys. People became edgy...they just did not want to enter into that conversation". Valerie a principal noted:

> Teachers and even other administrators are very reluctant to admit that race has any thing to do with an issue even when it is obvious. I cannot help my teachers to see that their behaviours is racist if we cannot even talk about it...I don't want to be the one that is always pointing out that racism is a factor. The students see the actions as racist...

A curriculum head in a large diverse secondary school with over ten years of experience said, "many educators are not culturally aware so there is a lack of understanding of how their thinking and behaviors are influenced by race, ethnicity and social class... I notice that the hardest issue to talk about is race". Few classrooms, schools, and school districts can point to educators who are truly willing and prepared to address racial issues (Singleton & Linton, 2006). Students and teachers need to process their experiences in the world as racial group members. Recognizing ways that race impacts our work is not to ask, "Am I a bad person?" Instead, it is to ask, "Do my everyday acts help promote a more equitable society?" (Pollock, 2008, p. 3). Pollock also writes:

> Everyday antiracism requires addressing people's experiences in the world as racial group members and refusing to distort people's experiences, thoughts, or abilities by seeing them only or falsely through racial lens. This applies when educators interact with students in classrooms, design and discuss curriculum, interact with students' families, or even think about ourselves and colleagues... Above all, educators must keep analyzing which of our everyday actions counteract racial inequality and which do not (Pollock, 2008, p. xix).

Racism cannot be swept under the rug. These issues must be addressed in schools if students of color are to feel safe, valued and respected. Gillian, an experienced principal noted:

> Many educators are not socio-culturally conscious. There is a lack of understanding of how their thinking, behaving and being in schools are influenced by race, ethnicity and social class…The willingness is not there to develop culturally competent teachers and programs because of the fear and discomfort of addressing race and racism in the classroom.

Khalifa, Gooden, and Davis (2016) echo this point. They argue that White school leaders are sometimes not aware of their culturally oppressive leadership practices because discussing race causes them discomfort. They suggest that school leaders of color and some administrators may also contribute to the further marginalization of students because they have not paid attention to their internalized oppression. In my own practice I have witnessed Black school leaders being unduly harsh on Black students because they fear being seen as complicit and playing "favorites with Black kids". Internalized oppression and racism is harmful not only to school leaders, but also to students, as they do not feel affirmed and valued in these environments (Harris-Tigg, 2005). Khalifa et al. (2016) suggest that:

> When school leaders reproduce racial oppression, a number of practices are visible, including internalized racial inferiority among administrators of color, embracing of the color-blind ideology, and maintaining questionable leadership preparation programs that minimize or exclude altogether meaningful conversations on race, culture, and community (p. 15).

Schools assist in the replication of dominant cultural values, and as such it is important that educators become aware of changes that are taking place in the world (White & Cooper, 2012). Administrators, teachers, students, and others involved in education must become involved in shaping the conversation of tomorrow especially as schools experience ever-increasing diversity and difference (Bates, 2001). Critical race theory (Aylward, 2000; Henry & Tator, 2009; Ladson-Billings, 2000) helps us to understand the impact of race in education and its impact in the teaching and learning process. Critical race theory includes experiential knowledge and narratives in developing critical understanding and analysis of the practices of educators (Solorzano & Yosso, 2001). The following elements are highlighted: (1) the intersectionality of race with other forms of oppression, (2) the challenge of the dominant ideology, (3) a commitment to equity and diversity, (4) the centrality of experiential knowledge, and (5) transdisciplinary perspective that are also key aspects of social justice and culturally responsive leadership practices that offer theoretical convergence (Solorzano & Villalpando, 1998; Solorzano & Yosso, 2001).

Through the voices of the school leaders represented in this research it is hoped that others will feel a sense of agency to take action, examine their practices, and become more active in how education is shaped for the future. Recognizing moments of tension can inspire the curiosity of school leaders and educators to learn and this can be exciting and energizing professionally and personally. Tensions provide a way of challenging our thinking and understanding experiences differently, creating curiosity. It is important that educational leaders harness moments of tension into action, moving from inspiration to influence. One school leader suggested that she handles tensions that she experiences by seeking out "avenues for action". Wrestling with tensions is not often encouraged in leadership practices and doing so publicly is sometimes discouraged (Feldman & Tyson, 2014). Tensions create spaces for critical reflection to occur and by contending with issues that impact leaders personally and professionally, aspiring leaders can begin to make sense of work situations in socially just ways which create avenues for change (Mullen, Young, & Harris, 2014). Bogotch and Reyes-Guerra (2014) argue that what is needed is for leaders to pedagogically unpack theories, grapple with tensions, and inspire a more socially just/antioppressive relationship among educators, students, and communities. Some African Canadian school leaders in the study raised the issue of coming to an understanding of ways that they themselves had internalized oppression, and had to navigate their own pain and the impact on their practice. According to Dei (1999), examining the inner self and our relation to the world and the community is important in how we look at educating young people.

Think Alouds—Questions for Reflection

1. What are some of the tensions that you experience on the job as a school leader?
2. How might school leaders begin to have 'courageous conversations' about race?
3. What might be some of the complexities on the journey as educational leaders navigate a path of critical praxis?
4. What are some additional ways that culturally responsive and socially just leaders might build capacity?

Research Activity

1. Critical Race Theory (CRT) has been posited by many social justice scholars as a way of understanding and deconstructing issues of race in society and education. Complete a literature review of CRT. How might CRT help school leaders to understand issues of race in current contexts?
2. Are schools effective in creating learning communities that buttress the tensions that leaders experience professionally and personally? How might schools as learning organizations become more proactive in dealing with this issue?

CHAPTER 5

Mentoring and Support—Collaborative Mentorship

School leadership is difficult and complex regardless of which theory undergirds the approach (Bogotch & Reyes-Guerra, 2014). Educational leaders in many Western countries are faced with the complexities of demographic and social change within schools and communities (Wilson-Forsberg, 2012). This shift has caused some educational leaders to experience heightened anxiety while serving diverse students and communities (Ham & Cormier, 2015). Contemporary school administrators play a number of roles ranging from educational leaders and change agents, to instructional leaders, curriculum and assessment experts, budget analysts, facility managers, special program administrators, and community builders (Davis, Darling-Hammond, Lapointe, & Meyerson, 2005).

Over the years the need for ongoing support for educational leaders has become more apparent, and assisting leaders is viewed as an important part of ensuring that they can be more effective (Daresh, 2004). It is important to examine ways that school leaders can be supported, mentored, and sustained as they wrestle with the complexities and challenges of schools. Bogotch and Reyes-Guerra (2014) suggest that "it is hard to be good at anything in education…It is understandable, therefore, why dedicated and committed educators who put all of their energies, mentally and physically, into building a good school would be hesitant—if not resistant-in confronting social injustices beyond their school buildings" (p. 2). The working conditions of school leaders are complex, the tasks daunting, and many suffer from burnout as mentioned in Chap. 4. Some school leaders

A.E. Lopez, *Culturally Responsive and Socially Just Leadership in Diverse Contexts*, DOI 10.1057/978-1-137-53339-5_5

feel unprepared to work with culturally and ethnically diverse students and communities and welcome support in this area. School leaders sometimes find it challenging to work in places of highest demand, especially in underserved communities and schools where working conditions are most challenging, (Knapp, Copland, & Talbert, 2003). Leaders must be trained and supported so that they can provide the environment where students will be successful (Leithwood, Seashore-Loius, Anderson, & Wahlstrom, 2004). Greater attention is now being paid to how school leaders are recruited and prepared. Some suggest that coursework in leadership preparation programs is outdated and out of touch with the challenges and complexities of today (Murphy & Vriesenga, 2004). From my earlier research with teacher leaders and my most current research with principals and teacher leaders, many suggest that they would benefit from mentoring and support as they deal with challenges in schools.

In this chapter I explore collaborative mentorship (Lopez, 2005, 2013) as a form of mentoring and support for educational leaders. The notion of collaborative mentorship emerged as a mentoring approach from research that I conducted with teachers (Lopez, 2005). Collaborative mentorship is theorized as a mentoring approach that focuses on supporting and sustaining educators to advance issues of equity and diversity grounded in critical dialogue and a dialogic relationship between mentor and mentee where opportunities are created for both to become vulnerable and wrestle with tensions (Lopez, 2005). Collaborative mentorship is undergirded by the notion that mentoring should be collaborative, with mentee and mentor being equals in the relationship. This disrupts the traditional mentoring roles of expert and protégé. The concept of mentoring goes back to the first telling of the mythical legend of a Mentor who was entrusted with the education of Odysseus' son, Telemachus (Adams & Scott, 1997). As the story goes, Mentor guides Telemachus on a journey in search of his father. Intrinsic to this tale is the idea that mentoring can be an intentional, nurturing, insightful, supportive, and protective process (Anderson & Shannon, 1988). Although the term "mentor" is rooted in mythology, it has grown and flourished throughout the history of education (Janas, 1996). Today mentors form an important part of the professional development of school administrators and educational leaders.

The role and impact of mentoring in education has a long history, and it has been well established as a successful tool of professional development. The heart of mentorship comes from a commitment to education, a hope for its future, and a respect for those who enter into its community

(Shadiow, 1996). Despite its prominence in education there is no fixed and rigid definition of mentoring and definitional diversity continues to characterize the field. Zey (1984) defines a mentor as "a person who oversees the career and development of another person usually a junior, through teaching, counseling, providing psychological support, protecting, and at times promoting and sponsoring" (p. 7). Zey also suggests that a positive mentoring relationship can benefit the organization in addition to those directly involved. Adams (1998), for example, defines mentoring as an integrated approach to enhance professional growth. Anderson and Shannon (2001) define mentoring as a nurturing process in which a more skilled or experienced person serves as a role model, teacher, counsellor, who encourages a less skilled person on a path of professional development. Wasden (1988) in defining mentoring suggests that "the mentor takes great pains to help the steward recognize and negotiate dangerous situations. In doing all this, the mentor has an opportunity for growth through service, which is the highest form of leadership" (p. 7).

In this new era of change and demographic shifts, mentoring is an important way of supporting and sustaining educational leaders in dealing with the changing situations that they face. Mentoring remains a viable policy option in education, but its complexity must be understood for purposeful mentoring to occur (Koki, 2011). Mentoring provides great potential as part of the socialization of aspiring and new school leaders (Daresh, 2004). As the field progresses, many in education now refer to the *mentoring relationship*, which signifies a collaborative effort. Over the years new mentoring epistemologies have emerged that have disrupted the traditional mentoring relationships characterized by expert and protégé given the issues of power that might exist in such relationships (Mullen, 2009). Alternative approaches to mentoring such as co-mentoring (Cohen, 2002), collaborative mentoring (Mullen, 2000), and feminist mentoring (David, 2008) have emerged in the literature in recent years.

School leaders in the study felt that they would benefit on their journey as culturally responsive leaders with the support and mentoring of other culturally responsive school leaders. One teacher leader suggested that she would benefit from a "network of leaders to collaborate with, and the opportunity to work with other leaders... I would not feel so alone sometimes". The feeling of being alone or feeling "like the only one" in the school taking on the complex issues diversity poses was a consistent concern raised by school leaders in the study. One principal suggested that "mentoring and supporting school leaders who are interested in culturally responsive leadership should be made a mandatory part of leadership training". She noted further that "Mentoring for culturally responsive leaders should be explicitly mandated and reflected in the Ontario Leadership Framework (OLF) and the Board's Leadership Framework". Another principal suggested that time "should be allocated so that those leaders interested in culturally responsive leadership can observe other leaders implementing those practices". Holloway (2004) argues that mentoring helps to relieve the stress that school leaders face on the job, such as dealing with varying stakeholders, the fast-paced environment, and the task of supervising teachers, and calls for well-structured mentoring programs that will ameliorate the isolation felt by new administrators. While Holloway focused mainly on newly appointed school administrators, what the study revealed about experienced school administrators who embrace a culturally responsive leadership approach, is that they too would benefit from mentoring and support.

Mentoring as Support and Sustenance—Collaborative Mentorship

As mentioned above collaborative mentorship validates the lived experiences of educators in a collaborative environment with the support of a mentor. Collaborative mentorship promotes collaboration between mentee and mentor in a relationship of equals where they learn from each other and take risks (Lopez, 2005). In this kind of mentoring relationship mentors not only guide, they make transparent their mentoring goals, try to understand the impact of their ideologies on the process, center social justice as their conceptual framework, engage in dialogue that promote empowerment, and transformation (Mullen, 2009). Issues of equity and diversity form the central theme in a collaborative mentoring relationship. The ultimate goal is to support the educational leader in becoming bold in taking risks, challenging forms of oppression, and confronting power structures that discriminate. This kind of mentoring is crucial to support those who take up the cause of critical work where dissonance might occur, particularly for those who are not from the same ethnic, cultural, and class background as the students they serve. While the student population is becoming increasingly diverse, those in educational leadership and classrooms remain predominantly White and middle class. As students from diverse racial, ethnic, and language groups seek access to educational opportunities in today's classrooms, it is important that educators be prepared to work effectively with diverse students (Ball & Tyson, 2011).

In the collaborative mentoring relationship, trust is important in creating nonjudgmental areas where both mentee and mentor can become vulnerable and engage on the journey of learning together. This is essential for the kind of transformative learning that sometimes needs to happen in order for practices to be changed where educators are on a journey to become more critical and culturally responsive. Sometimes the collaborative mentoring relationship can be difficult as this might involve unpacking one's own biases, stereotypes, assumptions, power, and privilege that might have only been superficially examined or not examined at all. In these instances and moments dissonance might be created and the support of a collaborative mentor becomes valuable. For example, White educators and school leaders who have not thought about the privilege that comes with their racial identity, sometimes struggle when issues of White privilege are being discussed, feel personally offended and uncomfortable. We know that from experience that through discomfort learning occurs. Talking about race and highlighting racism as one of the causes of oppression of ethnically and culturally diverse students seems to invoke, in some, deep discomfort and resistance. Many are reluctant to name race as a form of oppression even though racism is alive and well in education. As discussed in Chap. 4 racism is difficult for educators to talk about, and many educators tend to completely avoid conversations about race (Schwartz, 2014). It is important for school leaders not to leave racism to fester whenever it rears its ugly head but to take on and vigorously disrupt stereotypical and racist viewpoints (Ryan, 2006).

Tenets of Collaborative Mentorship

Drawing on my research with administrators and teachers, I theorize collaborative mentorship in ways that hyperbolize and enrich culturally responsive and socially just educational leadership theory and practices. I posit the following tenets as important in the collaborative mentoring relationship: (1) critical understanding of diversity and equity, (2) critical space for dialogue, (3) practical forms of support, and (4) reflection and agency.

Critical Understanding of Diversity and Equity

Engaging in the work that needs to be done on behalf of diverse learners calls for a robust understanding of equity and diversity (Portelli, 2011). We are living in an era where equity, diversity, social justice, and culturally responsive and culturally relevant pedagogy have almost become buzzwords, with little occurring by way of real change in the lives of diverse students. Acknowledging that diversity exists without articulating ways to bring about change and meaningful actions that educators can engage in is inert knowledge and meaningless in the lives of students. A robust understanding of equity and diversity names the issues, whether they be classism, racism, homophobia, Islamophobia, or other forms of oppression, and articulates ways of rooting them out of schools and the practices of educators. Laminated equity that pays lip service to equity without real change will not work (Lopez, 2005, 2011, 2013). In many schools and places of work equity policies are laminated and boldy placed on walls and front entrance ways for many to see, but practices remain unchanged, riveted in dominant practices and ways of knowing. I refer to this as laminated equity. In a relationship of shared understanding, mentee and mentor engage in praxis that seeks to transform context and self, where critical knowledge about equity and diversity emerges. For example, as educational leaders engage in a collaborative mentoring relationship and begin to review think about critical proactive ways of dealing with diverse students they might begin to disciplinary practices and become more mindful of the circumstances that might prevent students from making better choices, instead of being focused on punishment. In other examples, different approaches to deal with truancy might emerge that involve the community in developing and implementing school policies in more sensitive ways.

Critical Space For Dialogue

The idea of critical space are safe spaces where mentee and mentor can become vulnerable in the collaborative mentoring relationship, where knowledge is co-constructed and co-laboring happens. In this critical space greater self-awareness is developed and blind spots are uncovered. Without self-awareness that includes understanding the biases one brings to a mentoring relationship, confronting one's own positions and prejudices, mentoring for equity and diversity is undermined (Achinstein & Athanases, 2005). In this critical space mentee and mentor are able to excavate deeply held views about issues, such as race. Tatum (2001) suggests that it is important to break the race taboo and overcome anxieties about exposing one's own internalized racism. These moments in a collaborative mentoring relationship require critical spaces. Critical space include physical space, and the activities that take place in that space which might include talking, sharing, laughing and silence and so on. Courageous discussions that include ideological and socio-political realities, personal experiences, and the tensions between these dynamics, while disturbing, are ultimately transformative (Solomon & Levine-Rask, 2003). According to Mayo (2002) safe spaces must be created in schools where dominant ideologies can be challenged and people become vulnerable. As the collaborative mentoring relationship develops and a critical learning community evolves, co-construction of knowledge becomes an ongoing process. Jehangir (2012) argues that a learning community is a space where tensions are wrestled with, social issues challenged, and new concepts emerge. Safe and critical spaces promote risk taking, disruption of beliefs and values, and create discomfort that leads greater learning (Gayle, Cortez & Preiss, 2013).

Practical Forms of Support

Educational leadership scholars, researchers, and practitioners continue to call for more explicit ways of bringing theory into action. Many ask what does it look like in practice? This is evident in the social justice and culturally responsive leadership literature. This is an area where a mentoring relationship that is built on trust and reciprocity can be helpful to school leaders who have to juggle many balls on a day to day basis. If change is to occur then we must continue to articulate ways that these theories can be implemented in schools and have real impact on the lives of students. In this effort a collaborative mentoring relationship can be useful in supporting educational leaders in a variety of ways which might be as simple as sharing of resources on equity and diversity so that the school leader can use her time in the pursuit of other activities. In a collaborative mentoring relationship sharing of resources is important as it can lead to the development of new knowledge and exposure to new ideas. This is a practical form of support that does not require a lot of investment of time and can have immediate benefits. These resources might include current articles and research on equity and diversity, case studies that school leaders could use in their own contexts, information about the community and so on. Resources that will help in developing understanding, while at the same time supporting school leaders in building capacity.

School leaders in the study identified a lack of resources to draw on as a challenge. They also noted that having or knowing the kind of resources to access saved valuable time given how busy schools are. Practical forms of support move beyond theorizing and offer comfort that although the work is challenging it is doable and workable. Mulford (2003b) suggests that well-supported leaders sustain improvements and increase their capacity. In the collaborative mentoring relationship this practical form of support could also involve collaborating on strategies to navigate the beauracracy. School leaders dealing with issues of equity and diversity might also need suppot in developing responses when faced with resistance and how to navigate dissent successfully minimizing personal and professional risks.

Reflection and Agency

It is important that school leaders become agentive and act on behalf of diverse students. Reflection is the cornerstone of any mentoring relationship and is important in informing practice. Through reflection educators begin to understand and problematize their practice, seeking solutions to difficult issues. In the collaborative mentoring relationship, reflection builds understanding of the possibilities for change. This can be beneficial to both mentor and mentee. This form of reflexivity examines how people are implicated in relationships.

Mentoring for equity and diversity requires skills and dispositions that support the building of a dialogic mentoring relationship where alternate knowledge emerges and critical consciousness is awakened. Both mentee and mentor thrive and grow in a community of learners. Positive relationships are built where learning and unlearning takes place. Collaborative mentoring relationships rupture existing ways of knowing and being, and require both mentor and mentee to be committed for it to be lasting and sustainable. The success of collaborative mentorship rests on the willingness of the mentor and mentee to be joint partners in the co-construction of knowledge and to engage in cultural border crossing where necessary. This kind of mentoring relationship can be emotionally charged as mentor and mentee border-cross identities, builds understanding and engage in reflective activites that are transformative. When educators engage in alternative discourses and practices that disturb a sense of cohesiveness, trauma can be provoked. This can cause anguish and pain (Nieto, 2002), and must be recognized (Britzman, 1998). The mentor must be cautious of not becoming a dominant voice in the relationship and take on the role of expert, thereby creating unhealthy power relations. Collaborative mentoring is a process that is flexible, and can become a means of support and sustenance for educational leaders on a path of critical praxis. It is a mentoring approach that supports school leaders on the job.

Mentoring can no longer be about duplicating past practices (Daresh, 2004). Daresh asserts that:

> Schools adopt the enhancement of diversity as a clear and consistent goal; mentors cannot simply pass a torch that is no longer consistent with the inclusion of new expectations for ethnic, gender, cultural, and racial diversity... this implies that the mentoring process must involve efforts to help new educational leaders gain insights into trends, issues and social realities (p. 512).

It is important for educators to understand themselves, their ideologies, philosophies, and their own identities. Increasing self-knowledge supports educators to more fully appreciate the diversity that exists and the cultures of their students (Santoro, 2009).

Actions To Support Collaborative Mentoring Relationship

In developing the collaborative mentoring relationship, while there is room for flexibility, it is important for both mentor and mentee to have a sense of the actions that guide relationship. The actions suggested below could be useful for practitioners and school leaders who are embarking on a collaborative mentoring relationship (Lopez, 2005).

- There must be trust between the participants so that space can be opened up where both can be vulnerable. For trust to develop there must be an ongoing relationship between mentee and mentor. Social justice work cannot be done in isolation or as a series of events–moment to moment. There must be some continuity in the process.
- The collaborative mentor must be accessible. While email and phone conversations are useful and welcomed in an era where technology makes communicating easy, the collaborative mentoring relationship requires face-to-face interactions from time to time so that a deep meaningful and understanding relationship can develop.
- Experiences must be shared collaboratively and in a spirit of equals. It is not just one person being vulnerable, telling their stories and sharing their vulnerabilities. Both mentor and mentee must engage in respectful dialogue, where sharing back and forth becomes the norm in the relationship. Engaging in dialogue and conversations about what it means to be a socially just and culturally responsive educator is an important element of the collaborative mentoring relationship.

Through dialogue understanding is teased out and meanings developed. Both mentor and mentee examine how they are implicated in the educative process and co-construct meaning together.

- The collaborative mentor must be empathetic. Through Nel Noddings' work and others' we have come to better understand the power of empathy and caring in education. Empathy helps us not to be judgmental, but to listen, learn, and validate the feelings of others.
- The collaborative mentor, in addition to acknowledging vulnerabilities, must acknowledge when they do not know and must also engage in building their own capacity. This speaks to the incompleteness of knowledge and the "loopiness" of the collaborative mentoring relationship. The term "loopiness" is used to signify the twists and turns that occur in the relationship over time.
- There must be more than talk. There should be modeling of what actions might look like. The power of modeling is valuable in all aspects of education. We know from teacher education that effective teaching involves modeling, where students are able visualize the concepts being shared. Research suggests that learning is more effective when we are able to translate ideas into actions that are discernable.
- Clearly defined goals should be outlined in the collaborative mentoring relationship. How these goals connect to culturally responsive and social justice should be clear. For example, the mentor could assist the mentee, who is aspiring to a leadership role, to identify leadership goals to work towards. Another goal might simply be to build relationships with colleagues who might be considered as allies.
- Collaborative mentors should support mentees to examine ways that social justice and culturally responsive approaches support broader school and system goals. It is important for new and aspiring leaders to be able to make those connections beyond their own sphere of influence. This is important as they take on greater responsibilities.
- Mentees in a collaborative mentoring relationship should be supported in circumstances when there is fear of reprisal, particularly mentess from marginalized groups. Collaborative mentors can support mentess in understanding how to navigate those contexts and take action that will be empowering. For example, becoming comfortable with being known as a culturally responsive educator, and developing emotional strength to deal with resistance and push back. It might be necessary for the collaborative mentor to provide examples of the kind of resistance to expect and ways that that mentees might repsond. Another example might be ways to

respectfully call out a colleague who is engaging in micro aggressions. We cannot assume that everyone know how to respond in these difficult circumstances.

- Celebrate successes along the way and use moments of setback for learning and growth. Not everyone everyone will buy in and progress will be sometimes slow. Leaders must be encouraged to recognize small victories as success, learn and grow from them. This can be challenging even for experienced school leaders who sometimes put a great deal of effort into a project that does not turn out well or the way they intended. For some school leaders, these moments can be traumatic and frustrating.
- Dedicated time must be set aside for collaborative mentor and mentee to meet. This creates consistency. While there will be flexibility, the collaborative mentoring relationship should not be ad hoc and accidental. Both mentor and mentee must work towards honoring the time commitment. If the mentor and mentee are not at the same location then dedicated time to connect becomes even more vital.
- Discuss early in the relationship the kind of resources that each person is willing to share and how. It can lead to mistrust if it is perceived that sharing is going in one direction only. What is possible and not possible must be signaled and negotiated up front at the start of the relationship.

These practical suggestions should also be buttressed by scholarly research and literature to support grounding and understanding.

How Do Educational Leaders Seek Support?

As educators we all need support on our journey and sometimes we are reluctant to acknowledge this for fear of being seen as vulnerable or not psssessiing the knowledge that is required for the role that we find ourselves in. In an era of accountabilty and an environment where educators are often criticized for the state of education sometimes school leaders are reluctant to admit that they need support and sustenance. I argue that support is crucial in sustaining a path of critical work. Obidah (2008) suggests the following questions be asked when seeking support: (1) For whom are you seeking support? (2) Is this to make you feel good about being in the school or is it about teaching those particular students? (3) Are you seeking support to better yourself for the job? I add to this the following (4) How will this support enhance my understanding? (5) What specific area do I need to be supported in? (6) How can I pay the support I receive forward? By answering these questions school leaders can begin to formulate the kinds of support necessary and where they might people who can assist them. Based on the narratives of the participants, and my experiences in schools, I offer some additional practical suggestions and insights on ways that school leaders might go about seeking support.

- Develop a list of critical friends. These could be people that you meet in class or at work. Make a note of their area of expertise. Do not be afraid to call on critical freinds for support, this could be in the form of time or resource. It might be possible to have more than one collaborative mentor in the mentoring relationship who supports different aspects of the journey. For people of color, it might mean having someone from your own cultural group as well.
- Take an inventory of areas of weakness and make a list of where there is room for growth, capacity building and the kind of professional development needed. Choose one or two areas to work on, keeping in mind that this is a process that will take time. Be generous with self on what can be achieved within a given time period.
- Create a plan to work with diverse students highlighting areas where more knowledge is needed, areas of discomfort and areas of strengths. Sometimes support is needed to better connect with diverse students. Some educational leaders are uncomfortable working with students from different cultures, not because they harbour biases, but because of fear of offending, or fear that they might say the wrong thing. In circumstances like these the tendency can be to retreat and avoid what might be perceived as difficult conversations. Seek support from people outside of your own group who are different from your own in order to gain authentic knowledge and understanding.
- Like Obidah (2008) I suggest that school leaders sometimes seek out and engage with what she describes as "feel good activities". These allow educators to focus on positives and enhance their effectiveness.

Collaborative mentorship offers school leaders a way of building capacity in spaces that are supportive recognizing that the path of critical education is difficult. If educators are to be effective with an increasingly diverse student population, they need to recognize and understand their own worldviews before they can appreciate and honor the worldviews of their students (McAllister & Irvine, 2000). Given the changing student population, there is an increasing need for culturally respectful approaches to teaching and learning where methods that engage one population of learners do not offend another (Lipton, Wellman & Humbard, 2003). The aim is to build common understanding where all voices will feel included and valued as week seek to create a more just society.

Think Alouds—Questions for Reflection

1. In what ways might collaborative mentorship assist you on your journey to become a culturally responsive and socially just school leader?
2. What kinds of mentoring support might be most useful to experienced school administrators?
3. What are some of the challenges that you might face in becoming a collaborative mentor?
4. How would you make the argument that mentoring specifically aimed at culturally responsive and socially just school leaders should be made explicit and mandatory in your board's or district's leadership framework?
5. As you peruse the tenets of collaborative mentorship, what might be added? What areas do you find challenging?

Research Activity

1. Mentoring has been present in education for a long time. How has it evolved in educational leadership? How might traditional notions of mentoring that foreground expert and protégé perpetuate hegemonic practices in schools? In what ways might this be disrupted?
2. How effective are schools as learning organizations in supporting the development of school leaders to be agentive and critical? How might mentoring become a viable way of dealing with resistance in schools?

CHAPTER 6

One One Cocoa Full Basket: Reflections on My Journey

My experiences as a Black woman born and raised on the island of Jamaica and an immigrant to Canada have impacted and informed my educational philosophy and journey. These experiences have a created a deep commitment in me to the causes of social justice in education and society at large. To work towards ensuring that all children have access to a just and equitable education, regardless of their location in the world (Lopez, 2016). Listening to the voices of school leaders who engage in culturally responsive practices will help to facilitate, unpack, and problematize institutional policies that are ingrained in leadership knowledge production (Arnold & Brooks, 2013). The transformative work of radical leaders who were "not afraid to confront, to listen, to see the world transformed (Freire 1970/1993, p. 21)" have impacted my own understanding and development as a teacher, scholar and researcher. My educational leadership experiences (teacher leader, school administrator and university administrator) have been gained at educational institutions in the Greater Toronto Area (GTA), Canada.

I bring to my role of educator and educational leader multiple and fluid identities. We are informed by the many aspects of our lives such as age, gender, socio-economic status, language, religion, race, sexual identity, and other forms of difference. My theoretical stance is that of a critical educator who argues for culturally responsive and socially justice approaches to education that challenge all forms of oppression and power in education.

A.E. Lopez, *Culturally Responsive and Socially Just Leadership in Diverse Contexts*, DOI 10.1057/978-1-137-53339-5_6

In this chapter I examine my experiences as an educational leader through my lens as a Black woman. However, doing so is not to the exclusion of other sites of oppression. As Dei (2008) argues, the foregrounding of race does not mean the exclusion of class, gender, and sexual orientation, as the lived experiences of those who face racism daily from others is one where they must also face inter/intraracial classism, sexism, and other forms of oppression. Dei also reminds us that:

> Social identities are constructed beyond notions of race, class, gender, sexuality, language and culture to the actual practices engaged by people in the course of daily interactions … our identities are made in social interaction in concert with and using categories of difference and identity. In order to effectively organize for political change, we first have to recognize and understand that identity is defined by who the individual is, how the individual self is understood in relation to others, and how such constructions of social identities match or do not match what people actually do in their daily lives … identity provides the basis for political struggle (p. 34).

Engaging in social justice leadership and culturally responsive leadership as a critical educator is a political act, and one needs to know the self in order to engage in political action, find out what needs to be done, and how to do it (Dei, 2008). As a critical social justice and culturally responsive educational leader I continue to seek out ways to bring theory to action, and create real change in how students, particularly those who have been marginalized and underserved, experience education in their classrooms and schools on a daily basis. I take me role seriously knowing fully well the obstacles that I will have to overcome and endure on the journey. While it is important to approach social oppression along multiple and shared dimensions of identity, to be a woman of racial minority background is to have even less material power and privilege in a patriarchal, White-dominated society (Dei, 2008).

My lived experiences as a racialized school leader have been filled with moments of learning and insights. My educational journey in Canada started as a secondary teacher in a large diverse school in the Greater Toronto Area. The school community was changing demographically with the influx of new immigrants. At the school where I started my teaching career in I was one of five minority teachers on a teaching staff of over one hundred. All the administrators were White at the time when I was hired. The student population was diverse, comprising of Asians, Blacks, South Asians from the Indian sub continent, South Asians from the Caribbean

(Guyana and Trinidad), and White students from various cultural backgrounds. The student population was a representation of the diversity that is reflected in Canada. After eleven years as a classroom teacher of Business Studies and Economics I became a vice principal in the same school where I was first hired as a teacher. I later transferred to another school in the same school board and city, where the student population was made up primarily of students who required alternate forms of education. Even though my educational leadership experiences include administration in higher education this chapter focuses on my educational leadership experiences in K9 - K12 contexts. It is an autobiographical narrative primarily of my experiences as a secondary school leader and administrator.

Through this autobiographical narrative I reflect on my journey as a culturally responsive and social justice school leader in K9-12 schools. Russo (1991) argues that self-reflective critique and the validation of personal experiences is part of the process of creating theoretical and practical knowledge for social transformation. The metaphor “one one cocoa full basket” is a Jamaican saying that my grandmother used frequently. This metaphor was often used by her to describe situations where patience was needed to accomplish a task. I have uses this metaphor as inspiration to keep going no matter what the challenges are, celebrating small successes along the way. Through this metaphor I am inspired to keep on my journey recognizing that change and often success can be slow and incremental. Major successes are achieved through small successes. Much of the work of critical educators could be exemplified through this metaphor. While there has been some change in schools in Canada and Western countries in implementing equitable strategies that focus on diverse students, more work needs to be done.

Autobiographies provide a retrospective framework through which we reconstruct our understanding of our journey within historical, social, and cultural frameworks (Schwalm, 2014). The position from which my story is rendered is that of a social justice and culturally responsive educational leader navigating a path of leadership that is filled with tension and possibilities, fully knowing that there is no end and final destination, but acknowledging the promise of the journey. Bamberg (2011) suggests that autobiographies are complex because they highlight dilemmas, uniqueness, and agency at the same time. Individuals must be able to critically reflect upon their own experiences and accumulated personal knowledge about the workings of the inner self and questions of identity, in order to work collectively for change (Dei, 2008).

Autobiographies allow us to be vulnerable as they position the self in relation to others through narratives (Schwalm, 2014) and become a form of social action as we make sense of our personal experiences (Slotadijk, 1978). Through this autobiography I reflect on and examine the ways that I seek to create change in the lives of diverse students from my position as a Black school leader and what that means as I engage with others. Through this process I have convergence of thought and bring my own experiences to bear on my understanding of what culturally responsive and social justice leadership might look like in schools. Like most autobiographies my journey is not linear, but instead consists of ebbs and flows. Through this autobiographical narrative I seek to understand my changing experiences and my journey as a critical educator highlighting what I see as important, and providing interpretations of the accounts (Roberts, 2002).

My narrative and story are subjective as these are my own experiences examined through my own eyes. The self-representation of the individual life or autobiography is not a new phenomenon but has developed as a cultural practice (Mascuch, 1997). Autobiography has been linked to the notion of subjectivity and personal identity. Through personal documents (Plummer, 2001) that include journal notes, personal tales, and memory I tell my story. As I tell my 'own story' I reflect on the successes and tensions as a Black school leader and educator. Santamarina and Marinas (1994) argue that autobiographical research has both an ethical and political dimension as memory is retrieved and narrated by the social actors themselves who use that as data to capture meanings and processes of construction of our individual identities. When we focus on our identities, how these are mediated through our voices as educators, how we are read and how we understand the world, autobiographical accounts allow for innovative critical perspectives as we navigate educational spaces (Jelinek, 1986).

Post-colonial approaches to autobiography have expanded the corpus of autobiographical writing and provided a perspective that is critical (Schwalm, 2014). Clandinin and Connelly (2000) draw attention to the power of narratives in understanding practice and suggest that. "experience is what we study, and we study it narratively because narrative thinking is a key form of experience and a way of knowing and thinking about it" (p. 18). When biography and history are joined, when the issue confronted by the self is shown to have relationships to and bearing on the context and ethos of a time, our narratives become a form of research (Bullough & Pinnegar, 2001). Theories are to be understood according to the narratives and theorization that takes place within specific contexts and problems (Denzin & Lincoln, 2000).

Traditional theories of educational leadership do not explicitly address issues of social justice and equity in schools. The kind of educational leadership that I research and advocate is one that is socially just and culturally responsive (Beachum, 2011; Bogotch, 2005; Bogotch & Shields, 2014; Furman, 2012; Jean-Marie, 2008; Ryan, 2006; Shields, 2010). Educational leaders who are socially just and culturally responsive take purposeful actions to bring about change in schools by ensuring that the various knowledges of diverse learners are included in the teaching and learning process. In doing so they challenge power structures, systems, and practices that continue to oppress and exclude some students.

For biographies to be powerful they must include what Graham (1989) refers to as 'modal moments'. These moments are central to teaching and learning where patterns of experience are recreated that allow for a reinterpretation of the lives and experiences of both the writer and the reader (Bullough & Pinnegar, 2001). As I reflect on my practice and my roles as teacher leader and school administrator there have been 'modal moments' that have allowed me to reflect deeply and rethink my position and stance as a critical educator and what I learned from those experiences that I draw on today. These instances include challenging other. There have been moments of dissonance between what the system, and even some colleagues, expected of me and my own critical educational philosophy that seeks to disrupt existing norms and challenges the status quo. There were moments of pain and uncertainty as I questioned myself and my role in implementing polices that had deleterious effects on students of color and marginalized students.

As an administrator I was responsible for enforcing discipline within the context of the *Safe Schools Act* that the Conservative government had implemented to deal with violence that occurred in schools. It was referred to as the "zero tolerance" policy to discipline which sought to punish students for any acts of violence without taking into account mitigating factors. The "zero tolerance" policy was constructed on the notion that a consistent set of guidelines was needed to govern what was deemed as unacceptable behaviour in schools where a set of predetermined rules were subsequently applied to determine the appropriate consequences and punishments for such behaviors (Holloway, 2002). Many argued that this policy had a devastating effect on special education students and students of color. Zero tolerance policies have come under intense criticism in Canada and the United States for advocating a blanket approach to addressing behavior problems, disproportionate adverse impact on students from minority groups and questionable effect on the overall safety and security of students

(Daniel & Bondy, 2008). According to Daniel and Bondy the Safe Schools Act (2001) in Ontario that was passed within a discourse of zero tolerance had a detrimental impact primarily on students of color. The Safe Schools Act dealt a blow to issues of equity especially for students of color and students with disabilities. As a school administrator I watched as students of color were arrested and suspended, knowing that this would negatively affect their chances of success in life. As a person of color whose history, identity, and experiences connect with the histories, identities, and experiences of the students impacted most neagitvely I felt very troubled at times.

In Ontario, the first steps toward taking a zero tolerance approach to discipline in schools began in the mid-1990s. The Conservative government made school safety a key issue in their platform, and zero tolerance policy for inappropriate behavior in schools came into being. This followed similar approaches to discipline in schools in the United States where standardized approaches to issues in schools were seen as the solution to problems. The *Safe Schools Act* was passed by the legislature in June 2000 and came into effect in September 2001. The *Act* brought in discipline that included full expulsion from all publicly funded schools in Ontario until the student completed the requirements of a strict discipline program, called Fresh Start. On paper, a fresh start sounded great and, being tough on crime with a focus on school safety, was appealing to the base of the Conservative party. I saw firsthand the devastating effects on parents and youth. Sitting in meetings with parents of children, who were often Black and Brown, being expelled or suspended for twenty days had a deep impact on me as a Black school leader who understands the impact of system racism and oppression in society and the role that implict bias plays in how some students experience school.

Sometimes I was rendered invisible, feeling that some expected me to behave and pretend as if I was not impacted at all. I must admit there were times I felt numb from the experience of what I was witnessing. Angry childish outbursts in the cafeteria where punches were thrown between students became police investigations, instead of involving restorative discipline approaches that allowed students to see their mistakes and change their behaviors. When schools enforce severe disciplinary consequences for minor infractions, it isolates students, and they feel abandoned at a time in their developmental continuum when they most need support (Sughrue (2003). In the USA research found that zero tolerance discipline in schools disproportionately impacted students of color (Casella, 2003; Cooper, 2000; Hoffman, 2005). The Ontario Human Rights Commission in 2003 launched an investigation into the effects of the Ontario Safe Schools Act and the impact zero tolerance policy on racialized youth. The report contained vivid details of racialized students being unfairly charged with crimes and supported what many had believed for a long time that the Act unfairly targeted students of color.

Kovalenko (2012) in her study of the impact of zero toleance on minority students argues that discriminatory institutional practices and the lack of appropriate support structures for immigrant youths and their families with respect to the Canadian educational system, make it challenging for racialized immigrant youths to be successful in education. These students she notes are more likely to be linked to the Canadian Criminal Justice System. Due to complaints from parents who felt that their children were being unfairly targeted under the *Safe Schools Act*, the Ontario Human Rights Commission filed a formal complaint against the Toronto District School Board (TDSB). In 2005 that probe looked into disciplinary policies at the Board, the Ontario Safe Schools Act, TDSB disciplinary policies and their impact on racialized youths. It was found that the *Act* was having a disproportionate effect on racialized students and students with disabilities, and that the Board failed to meet its legal obligations in the application of discipline partially because it provided inadequate education support services for suspended or expelled students (Mosher, 2008). The TDSB was forced to examine its policies, implement reforms on how racialized students were being disciplined, and provide cross-cultural training so that staff could recognize and avoid racial profiling and stereotyping. The Board also sought to recruit more teachers from racialized groups (Mosher, 2008).

It is important to note that racialization is not only about race; it includes other aspects of identity such as immigrant status, ethnicity, class, and gender (Anthias, Yuval-Davis, & Nira, 1993). Racialization is a process of categorization through which social relations between people are structured by the signification of human biological characteristics in ways that define and construct differentiated social collectivities (Miles, 1989). Miles also suggests that the concept of racialization is not fixed or static, but fluid and changes over time and place. Scholars over the years have built on Miles' notion of racialization to include ways that racialized identities are lived and self-identified in response to hegemonic and community constructs of race (Teelucksingh, 2006). According to Tanovich (2006), some teachers and school administrators do not realize that they are engaging in discrimination when they discipline racialized students more harshly or at a higher rate. Ruck and Wortley (2002) found that racial and ethnic minority students were much more likely than White students to perceive discrimination with respect to teacher treatment, school suspension, and the use of police by school authorities when dealing with incidents in school. The study also found that Black students were most likely to feel that they are being discriminated against, followed by South Asians, Asians, and students with lower socio-economic status. The Ontario Human Rights Commission (2007) noted that the impact of the zero tolerance disciplinary policies in schools had a devastating impact on racialized youths undergirded by issues of race, socio-economic status and poverty, and immigrant status. Many scholars have argued that the impact of zero tolerance discipline on students in Ontario might have been worse than reported, as Ontario for many years did not collect data on students based on race. Even though Ontario no longer has a "zero tolerance" policy, the issue of unfair and unequal discipline of racialized youth continues as evidenced by a survey report conducted by the TDSB in 2006/2007 that showed suspension rates were highest for Aboriginal students, followed by Black and mixed-race students. Despite well meaning efforts of some educators and policy makers these issues persist in the Ontario educational system today, at levels including higher education. We must remain vigilant and engage in activism to challenge these systemic issues.

Like Appleton (2011) I aim to locate, name, acknowledge and bring to the surface the often unvoiced elements of ourselves; the different ways we bring our authentic self and integrate our heart and soul into our work. As a social justice and culturally responsive school leader I seek ways to react to the pain and trauma that I feel and that have impacted me both professionally and personally. I challenge injustices upfront and publicly and continue to do so. As a school leader in two secondary schools in Ontario I was troubled by the inability of many parents to navigate the system and advocate for their children's education and rights. For example, some parents were not au fait with the process on how to appeal a suspensions given to their child. This impacted their ability to effectively advocate for their children. Achieving equity is about identifying and attempting to address structural disadvantage, discrimination and inequality. There were times as an administrator that I felt fearful of being seen as soft on discipline and particularly on students of color because I am Black. I was both fearful and courageous at the same time and this created professional and personal tensions. I grew in my role as a school administrator, I became more empowered and bold over time in challenging oppressive practices that I witnessed or experienced.

This is not a journey that anyone can take alone. I sought out allies and critical friends who were crucial in developing a community of support and learning. The notion of having critical friends, thoughtfully selected, is important. (Appleton, 2011). At times my professional knowledge was challenged or dismissed outright by White teachers who had less years of service or were blatantly racist. This type of 'othering' is not new in how racialized bodies are treated in the education system as we struggle to create spaces for counter-hegemonic storying (Davies, 2000). Racism has historically and continuously shaped the context and emotional possibilities for racialized bodies (Saldanha, 2006). Over the years the voices and epistemological practices of the dominant in education have sought to silence and render irrelevant the voices and experiences of Black people and people of color in public schooling (Ladson-Billings, 2000). By reflecting on my experiences I seek to disrupt the dominance of the Eurocentric ways of knowing and understanding in educational and school leadership. I seek to posit new discourses and epistemologies that emphasize new ways of knowing, rethink, re-strategize and reconstruct education which decenters Eurocentric ways of knowing as the primary source of knowledge in schools (Dei, 2000). I was once told by a White teacher who stormed into my office angrily that how my support of "certain" students was impacting the tone and discipline in the school because I dared to ignore his advice on the best way to discipline a Black student that he had provoked to anger and persistently harassed in the hallway for various minor infractions. I saw firsthand how quickly students of color were removed from the classroom, sent out of class to the office or the behaviorial room because some teachers could not be bothered to deal with the issues in the classroom or exercise a deeper level of patience.

There were times I felt like an outsider in a school system that paid lip service to equity on a macro level, while the status quo remained intact at the micro level. I was not fully prepared as a racial minority school leader to traverse the difficult and tension-filled conversations about race that often occur in schools (Cho, 2011). I had not anticipated the feelings of pain and trauma that such moments would evoke. At times I felt angry and anxious and worn down by the racist attitudes toward me from some staff members. Sometimes as racial minorities we are afraid of expressing how we feel because we are fearful of being accused of playing the race card. We suppress the pain we feel. It is important for Black and racialized bodies to engage with our experiences at both the practical and the emotional level. This is empowering professionally and healing personally.

Studies have shown that the impact of racism is harmful (Harrell, Hall, & Talieferro, 2003; Ogbu, 2003; Utsey & Ponterotto, 1996). It is important to examine, theorize, and come to an understanding of ways to be empowered and carry on the the important work challenging the staus quo and dominant knowledge. Obidah (2008) suggests that it is important to continue to overtly fight against oppression and acts of injustice, and when this happens the "second-guessing of self lessens and the 'self' as witness is empowered" (p. 57). Obidah goes on to say that anger is a powerful emotion that fuels the oppressed from victim to a position of empowerment and freedom. It is this empowerment that propelled me to forge ahead drawing on the examples of the great resisters of Jamaican history such as Marcus Garvey, Nanny of the Maroons, and Paul Bogle, as well as Nelson Mandela and others.

As a classroom teacher and teacher leader I approached teaching and learning from culturally responsive and antiracist perspectives that name, disrupt and transform existing structures of oppression (Dei, 2000; Henry & Tator, 2006; Irvine & McAllister, 2008; James, 1994; Ladson-Billings, 1995a; Lee, 2009). These were 'modal moments' for me as a classroom teacher as I sought to understand the complex and specific ways that racism operates in schools at the structural and personal level and develop strategies and actions to combat. One thing that was important to me was to build positive relationships with students. I had high expectations of them and demanded academic excellence. Ware (2006) refers to this as warm demander pedagogy. Warm demanders communicate both warmth and a non-negotiable demand for student effort and mutual respect. Researchers (See Cushman & Rogers, 2008; Bondy, Ross, Gallingane, & Hambacher, 2007) have suggested this approach is useful sustaining academic engagement in urban schools, and schools with large minority populations it is important to resist. One way of resisting is by engaging in various micropolitical activities.

Engaging in micropolitical activities that include "communicating and facilitating, collaborating, and using pressure and support" (Armstrong, Tuters, & Carrier, 2013, p.123) is important in forging alliances in order to create change. It was important for me to forge alliances with like minded teachers and sympathizers in moving a social justice agenda forward. Change can be created at many levels even through activities that we find challenging. Black History Month celebrations are one of those activities for me. While I see the short term benefits of Black students seeing their culture being honored I am troubled by the fact that Black History is only acknowledged once per year. The history and contributions of Black people should be embedded in the history books and taught at all levels of the curriculum. In one school planing Black History Month celebrations with students highlighted the importance of engaging in conversations with teachers and students about how notions of culture are understood and the continued importance in critical approaches to teaching and learning. I recall on one occasion how perplexed some of my colleagues and I became when some teachers decided to send only sent only Black students from their classes to attend the Black History Month celebration that was taking place in the auditorium. I recall with joy the rendition of the Black anthem by a choir made of students from various backgrounds and identities and how proud the students felt. It was joyful to showcase the contributions of the Black community, and watch the students participate with pride, while at the same time feeling saddened that some White teachers could not see the relevance of the event to their personal and professional growth as well as that of their students. This is in keeping with DiAngelo (2011) who suggests that because Whites live primarily segregated lives in a white-dominated society, they receive little or no authentic information about racism and are thus unprepared to think about it critically or with complexity. DiAngelo argues further: "the belief in objectivity, coupled with positioning white people as outside of culture (and thus the norm for humanity), allows whites to view themselves as universal humans who can represent all of human experience. This is evidenced through an unracialized identity or location, which functions as a kind of blindness; an inability to think about Whiteness as an identity or as a "state" of being that would or could have an impact on one's life" (p.59).

As a classroom teacher was imporant for me to use the curriculum as a space to disrupt dominant knowledge and perspectives about marginalized people and to positively showcase the contributions of Blacks and other racial minority groups. This was not foregrounded in the curriuculum and texts and to a large extent remains that way today. I recall an activity where students had to research inventions by female inventors who belonged to other racial and ethnic groups other than White. I discovered along with my students that the Sure Shot dispensing system that dispenses cream into coffee cups in many coffee shops in Canada was invented by a Black man. To this day when I share this information many students and people are surprised even though so many people drink coffee on a daily basis in Canada. The students were amazed that the inventors of color and women that we discovered in our classroom activity were not in their textbooks and most importantly not taught in their classes. I used various classroom activities to challenge students to think critically, develop socio-political consciousness and examine issues of issues of poverty, the environment, racism, and and other forms of oppression. As Giroux (1992) suggests teaching is inherently politcal. Gay (2013) reminds us: “the education of racially, ethnically, and culturally diverse students should connect in-school learning to out-of-school living; promote educational equity and excellence; create community among individuals from different cultural, social, and ethnic backgrounds; and develop students' agency, efficacy, and empowerment (p.49)”. By “politicizing the curriculum” (Montano, Lopez-Torres, DeLissovoy, Pacheo, & Stillman, 2002), possibilities are created for students to engage in conversations about what is possible for themselves and ways that power structures in education affect their lives.

As I reflect on my journey I have developed and gained a deeper understanding of what it means to navigate complex school environments. I am supported on this journey by critical friends and my own commitment not to give up even when the journey becomes tough. There are moments of powerlessness and fear sometimes to act, but as we progress on our journey we grow stronger, develop agency and deeper feelings of empowerment. Culturally responsive leadership and social justice leadership is a process that involves continuous learning and unlearning, and raises complex questions about the roles and responsibilities of school leaders. The tension between learning and unlearning, and realigning one's professional identity within our contexts, is an important story to tell by school leaders. There is an urgency for educational leaders of color to examine ways that school spaces are navigated, find opportunities and situations to act, understand when to be patient, and remain focused on their goals. Schools and universities are contexts are occupied by predominantly White bodies and as such discomfort will prevail as issues of race are dicussed and examined from the perspectives of Black and other racialized bodies. In a dominant society, interruption of racial belonging is rare and thus destabilizing and frightening to whites. White people often believe that multicultural / anti-racist education is only necessary for those who interact with “minorities” or in “diverse” environments. It is critical that all white people build the stamina to sustain conscious and explicit engagement with race (DiAngelo, 2011). On this journey I have learned to: engage in purposeful praxis and agency, take joy from small victories, seek out allies and critical friends, develop cross-cultural understanding, build bridges with parents and families, create space to include the voices of parents and students, build relationships develop a sense of empowerment be agentive. Despite the challenges it is an imperative that those in leadership in schools no matter their location (administration, teacher leader) continue to work towards change. Alternative frameworks aimed at understanding leadership that include alternative theories and practices, and disrupt taken-for-granted assumptions of what leadership is, what it can do, and what purposes it serves are needed (Young & Lopez, 2005). In moving from resistance to equity, educators encounter transformative possibilities (Solomon & Levine-Rasky, 2003) that must be used as learning moments.

Not all of my moments of learning as a school leader have been captured in this chapter. No one chapter or piece of writing will capture all moments of learning on any journey. In that regard it is incomplete. When educators engage in alternative discourse and practices that challenge our sense of cohesiveness, trauma is evoked (Britzman 2003). My experiences have taught me to develop agency and think critically how to navigate my educational contexts. As a critical social justice and culturally responsive educational leader my identity as a Black woman informs my work. As a Black woman growing up in Jamaica I have reflected on my own racial identity development and how that has informed my journey. While conversations about the impact of slavery and colonization were raised, naming racism was not evident in the British curriculum that were taught in schools. Upon migrating to Canada I experienced racism first hand which caused me to think about my own racial identity development and how I understood and interpreted the impact of racism on my own life. I found Cross (1991) stages of Black racial identity development useful. Cross (1991) identifies five stages of Black racial identity development: Pre-encounter, Encounter, Immersion/Emersion, Internalization, and Internalization-Commitment.

In the pre-encounter stage identification with White people takes place and Black culture is devalued. In the encounter phase there is emotional and personal experiences that bring about change. The Immersion/Emersion stage is marked by identification with Black culture. During the Internalization phase defensiveness is overcome, the effectiveness of racism is understood and Black identity is affirmed. The commitment stage sees Black identity embraced and various forms of oppression are resisted. Over the course of my time as a school leader in K9-12 schools I have traversed these stages in some way, shape, or form. As Cross indicates, these stages are not linear, but spiral and circular as we move back and forth based on our experiences. At the stage of internalization and commitment we find ways to translate our "personal sense of Blackness into a plan of action or a general sense of commitment" which is sustained over time (Cross, 1991, p. 220). The process of Internalization allows the individual to be anchored in a positive sense of racial identity and to become proactive where Blackness becomes the point of departure for discovering the universe of ideas, cultures, and experiences (Cross, Parham, & Helms, 1991). As we work as critical educational leaders to transform schools, in order to border cross we must develop a healthy and positive understanding of self and our own identity.

Racial identity development is also for White people and is an ongoing process of coming to understand their own privilege and the benefits of Whiteness. Regardless of our different identities and social location, critical social justice and culturally responsive educational leaders are allies in the struggle together to bring about change. Christine Sleeter (2008) reminds White people that they are "always beneficiaries of racism" (p. 93) and that the road of critical work is a difficult one. Sleeter suggests, "no matter how aware we [White people] are, we sometimes fail to notice privileges we receive; we sometimes miss opportunities to intervene or support…yet, for White people, the alternative is becoming bystanders who tacitly accept White supremacy as well as other forms of oppression. There is no comfortable way to grapple with race and racism" (p. 93). Conversations about Whiteness might best happen within the context of a larger conversation about racism and cannot be ignored. DiAngelo (2011) suggests that it might be useful to start at the micro level of analysis, and move to the macro, from the individual out to the interpersonal, societal and institutional. Starting with the individual and moving outward to the ultimate framework for racism – allows for the pacing that is necessary for many white people for approaching the challenging study of race. In this way, a discourse on Whiteness becomes part of a process rather than an event (Zúñiga, Nagda, & Sevig, 2002).

I am mindful of not reducing my experiences as a Black woman to a Black/White binary, recognizing that schools and classrooms are filled with diversity across all sections of identity and experience. Freire (1970) calls on critical educators to not be afraid to call out and name injustice that we see and engage in acts to promote social justice. As I reflect on my own journey as a critical educational leader, the need to translate educational theory into action in schools and classrooms is great. This has been the call by many social justice leadership scholars, such as Ira Bogotch, Gaetane Jean-Marie, and Jim Ryan. Teachers and school leaders committed to teach and lead in culturally responsive ways have shown examples from practice that others can draw on. While educational leaders are beginning to offer practical ways that social justice leadership can be practically implemented in schools, there is a long way to go in bridging the theory—practice divide.

Education has a tremendous role to play in society and must build awareness and articulate a future that is grounded in the material, emotional, and spiritual needs of our lives (Shapiro, 1995). Education must be in service of democracy, which is never final, but always in flux and under constant theoretical and practical negotiation. Solomon and Levine-Rasky (2003) urge all those working toward social justice to join forces to further the cause on behalf of marginalized students. We must develop a community where a deeper sense of "bonding and caring" can develop and where tensions are recognized and ideological and philosophical differences do not disappear (Nieto, 2002). Learning to work together toward social justice is important for all educators. Dei (1999) suggests:

> There is no way we can talk about education today which is anything but antiracist, anti-sexist, anti-classist. Antiracist education is good for everyone, not just minorities...It is good for the teacher, it is good for the administrator, it is good for the policy maker, because how we come to understand our world is powerfully connected to how we make sense of our existence in society" (p. 5).

The landscape of transformation as (Dyson, 2007) suggests, allows us to be in a state of becoming where we connect the multiple layers of our lives and consciousness, connecting the personal to the cultural. "We reach a stage when we begin to see things differently to that which we first thought, or perceived. Our prior perspective is turned upside down. Within this landscape we potentially live differently because we have seen another way of looking at the world and 'others' within the world in which we live" (Dyson, 2007, p.46). In telling our stories and drawing on images from our journey like boats on a stream, our narratives have the potential to move both author and readers to action.

Think Alouds—Questions for Reflection

1. Using a metaphor, describe your journey as an educational leader.
2. How would you characterize your own racial identity development?
3. How might school policies in your school or district, particularly those on discipline, be improved to reduce the possibilities of negatively impacting minoritized students?
4. As a social justice and culturally responsive educational leader describe the kinds of activities that you engage in within your context.
5. If social justice leadership is conceptualized as a journey and a continuum, where would you place yourself on this continuum? What kind of actions and supports might you need to move along your journey?
6. What advice would you give school administrators and school leaders seeking to implement culturally responsive leadership approaches to deal with personal and professional challenges they might encounter on their journey?

Research Activity

1. Drawing on current research, develop an action plan for administrators in a school district seeking to change its disciplinary policies to be more culturally responsive.
2. As a school leader, using a qualitative research approach write a biographical narrative of your journey as a school leader or administrator.

CHAPTER 7

Imagining Possibilities

A lot of change has occurred in the Jamaican education system, and education systems all around the world. Parents, educators, students, and communities have fought to make education a right and not a privilege. Today the discourse and dialogue in education is about how best to serve the needs of all students, particularly those students who have traditionally been underserved, how to integrate technology as a positive pedagogical tool, and how to respond to the massive demographic shift that is taking place and impacting societies everywhere. Educators who embrace a critical approach continue to call for education that challenges the status quo, and includes the experiences and identities of students and communities who have been excluded or marginalized, and for teaching approaches that are culturally responsive to the students and their communities. Parents, particularly those of children whose experiences in school have been beset with disengagement and underachievement, imagine an education system that is inclusive, culturally responsive, and socially just.

Dewey (1938) argued that a good education should benefit both society and the individual. He stated that there should be a societal purpose, and a purpose for the individual student. School leaders play a crucial role in creating schools that are responsive to the needs of diverse learners, which is what this book is about. According to Singer and Pezone (2003), citizens in a democratic society need to be critical and imaginative thinkers. John Dewey in *Experience and Education* urged educators looking for a new paradigm in education to think in terms of the deeper and larger issues of education.

A.E. Lopez, *Culturally Responsive and Socially Just Leadership in Diverse Contexts*, DOI 10.1057/978-1-137-53339-5_7

Demographic shifts and changing social realities have placed greater urgency on school leaders to be proactive in responding to the changes taking place in schools. Dewey suggested among other things that: (1) educators must make education relevant to the lives of students and place value on experiential learning; (2) teachers must engage in praxis—translating theory into action in ways that students can understand in their classrooms and schools; (3) educators must take into account the unique differences of each student in the teaching and learning process; (4) students have different past experiences and identities that make them unique; (5) each student will have a different set of experiences in response to the pedagogical methods used, even when these methods are standardized; (6) teaching, learning, and the curriculum must be designed in ways that allow for the individual differences of students to shine. Schools must be one of the places where the construction of a democratic community is worked on, and must be in the lead in building upon the diversity within their walls; and when this is achieved, the school, the community, and the nation benefits (Dewey, 1964). Dewey also noted:

> Are we entirely free from racial intolerance, so that we can pride ourselves upon having achieved a complete democracy? Our treatment of the Negroes, anti-Semitism, the growing serious opposition to the alien immigrant within our gates…What are our schools doing to cultivate not only merely passive tolerance that will put up with people of [difference]? What are our schools doing positively, aggressively and constructively to cultivate understanding and goodwill which are essential in a democratic society? (p. 42).

Dewey wrote this in 1964, but it could well have been written in 2016, as the very same issues are being debated and discussed in education and society today. Immigrants are being maligned, and positioned as threats to the fabric of American society by some who cling to the bigotry of the past. I imagine a future for culturally responsive and socially just education filled with possibilities, framed within Deweyean and Friereian models of education and building on the work of critical education scholars such as (Banks, 2009; Dantley, 1990; Dei, 1996; Foster, 1989; Giroux, 1992; Ladson-Billings, 1998; Lee, 2009; McLaren, 1995) and others. As educators, we choose how to view the world the lenses and philosophy that guide our work. As critical educators we must examine our assumptions and explore possibilities as we make choices about our practice (Hinchey, 2008).

Maxine Green stated that imagination is the cognitive capacity that allows us to break with the taken-for-granted, and transcend the familiar, a mode of thinking that refuses compliance, and helps us to look down the road not yet taken. What then do I imagine as possibilities for the future as a culturally responsive and socially just school leader? While the changes that are required in schools to meet the needs of all learners, and in particular diverse learners, are many, I highlight a few areas that are of great importance to me, as a call to action: (1) Diversity of teaching and administrative staff; (2) Increased allocation of resources; and (3) Embedding culturally responsive and socially just practices in leadership, teaching and learning.

Diversity of Teaching and Administrative Staff

Scholars of color, educational leaders, and others have placed diversification of the teaching force front and center in the educational discourse brought on by changes in the population and the glaring differences between teachers and the students they serve (Cole, 1986; Irvine, 1988). Research continues to point to the fact that diverse students do better in school when they see educators who share similar experiences and identities (Cole, 1986; Dee, 2005; Gordon, 2000; Irvine, 1988; Noguera, 2008; Villegas, Strom, & Lucas, 2012). While the student population is changing, those in the front office and at the front of the classroom remain predominantly White. Although some White teachers utilize effective pedagogy and make strong efforts to be culturally responsive and connect with diverse and minority students, research shows that students of color benefit when they have contact with teachers who look like them (Villegas et al., 2012). In my own experience as a classroom teacher and school administrator, on occasions too numerous to count I have had students walk up and say to me, "you are the first Black teacher that I have had" or "Miss, it is so nice to see a Black teacher". I have had the same experiences as a school administrator. This is in keeping with Miller and Endo (2005), who argue that as students of color they were inspired by teachers of color who served as excellent role models for them. The presence or absence of educators who share similar identities implicitly conveys information to students about the possibilities for their futures (Ogbu, 1991). Students pursue what they imagine as possible if they see a teacher or school administrator who shares their identity and experience. They will begin to imagine possibilities for themselves. Cole (1986) suggests that when students of color see examples of successful people who share similar identities it gives students hope and something to aspire to. A diverse teaching and administrative staff does not only benefit students of color and diverse students it also benefits White students as they become exposed to different perspectives. White students also benefit from a racially/ethnically diverse teaching force (Villegas et al., 2012).

The idea that teachers of color act as role models, and that efforts should be made to increase their presence in the teaching profession, builds on the idea that schools function to shape students' values as well as create academic success (Villegas et al., 2012). Representation matters and sends powerful messages about who is valued in the schooling space. Many scholars argue that the presence of different ethnic and racial groups helps to counter negative stereotypes. They also and act as mentors and cultural translators for students of color. When students fail to see minority adults in professional positions and instead see them overrepresented in the ranks of menial labourers and non-professional workers, they implicitly learn that it is normal for White people to be in positions of authority and people of color not (Villegas et al., 2012). We know from research that students of color are punished more frequently than White students, and hence it is important not to perpetuate the feelings of isolation and alienation that some feel in school.

Many colleges and universities in countries with large diverse populations have begun to take steps to increase the diversity of the teaching population, racially as well as in terms of class, sexual identity, and ability. All of the school leaders of color in the study, who were teachers, reflected on how important it was for them to act as role models to their students, a role that they took very seriously. One school administrator recalled when she was a resource teacher in a very large school board in the Grand Toronto Area (GTA), how important it was to her when a student ran up to her in the hallway and said, "Miss, do you work here, I want to be a teacher just like you". She had only immigrated to Canada a few years earlier from her home country and was still coming to terms with being a "racial minority" in Canada and what that meant for her as a teacher. Gay (2000), Villegas and Lucas (2004) and a growing body of scholars point to the importance of culture in the schooling experience of diverse students. Culture within this context is not understood from an essentialized and static position, but in ways that different communities go about expressing their interests and values in the world, which are fluid and changing. Teachers who are not from the dominant group bring to the teaching profession experiences and knowledge that are different, and connect students to multiple identities and experiences. They also bring knowledge and insights of ways that oppression and discrimination manifest in society (Quiocho & Rios, 2000).

Villegas et al. (2012) argue that "learning, far from being a personally passive act of receiving objective knowledge, involves the active construction of ideas within cultural contexts" (287).

An important aspect for diverse students, and those concerned with foregrounding their educational needs, is achieving academic success, as this more often than not is the only ticket to a life with a decent job and the ability to participate fully in society. Some scholars have argued that teachers of color have a unique role in challenging minority students to think about the importance of success in school and to make concerted efforts to achieve. I have experienced this first hand in both secondary schools that I have worked in the GTA, where I was able to have what I called the straight/firm/loving (SFL) talk with students of color about the importance of attendance, engagement, and achievement, much in the vein of what Ware (2006) calls the warm demander. Researchers are now pointing to the decline in the numbers of teachers of color, primarily of African American teachers as a cause for concern in the USA. Villegas et al. (2012) in their research found that African American teachers as a group "experienced a loss in their share of the overall teaching force despite a 27 % growth in their numbers overtime" (p. 296). They argue that more needs to be done to recruit minority teachers. I argue that more needs to be done in Canada as well to increase the diversity of teacher candidates entering teachers college with a view to diversifying teaching staffs in school. With an increasingly multiracial, multi-faith, multilingual and multicultural student population in the Canadian education system, teachers within the field and entering the field do not reflect this dynamic. The demographic make up of teacher candidates in teacher education programs remain white, middle class, heterosexual and female (James, 2007; Solomon, Portelli, Daniel & Campbell, 2005). Despite efforts progress is slow in this regard. In Ontario, the TDSB has collected data on the racial composition of the students and staff; however, other school boards are only just catching up. For example, the Peel District School Board, one of the largest school boards in Canada, has just started collecting racial data. More research is needed on the diversity of teacher candidates in teacher education programs and the impact of their efforts to recruit and diverisfy the teacher candidate pool. School boards should also report on their efforts to diversify their teaching staffs. Unless the data is made available we will not know the progress that is being made or lack thereof.

There is much less in the extant research on the diversity of administrators and those in positions of leadership in schools. Principal preparation programs must address the need for more diversity in school administration and pay greater attention to ways that school leaders can effectively and practically address issues of diversity in schools. There is need for more scholarship in the area of administrator preparation (Murphy & Vriesenga, 2004). According to Capper, Theoharis, & Sebastian (2006) in order to prepare leaders for social justice and the complex and shifting nature of schools, educational leadership programs must attend to critical consciousness, knowledge, and practical skills focused on social justice with their students. This is crucial if school leaders, and in particularly school administrators, are to develop the capacity and confidence to deal with the variety of students and experiences that they bring to school. Ryan, Pollock, and Antonelli (2007) in their research conducted in Canada argue that the need for diversity in the ranks of teachers as well as administrators is both an ethical and a practical matter. They suggest that administrators occupy a superior position in school hierarchies and greater diversity will have an impact on students, a view that is supported by other researchers (Branch, Hanushek, & Rivkin, 2013; Khalifa, 2013; Khalifa, Gooden, & Davis, 2016; Riehl, 2000).

Issues of difference and diverse students cover a broad range of research by scholars who focus on different aspects of diversity. Some scholars, like Lyman and Villani (2002), focus on poverty and leadership, and argue that future leaders need to understand the complexity of poverty. Solomon (2002) research in Canada, looked at antiracism in leadership preparation programs, and argued that school leaders need to understand how racism works as a system of oppression. Solomon advocated that school leaders need to learn how their own racial identity development impacts their leadership practice. Capper et al. (2006) challenged those preparing future school leaders. They suggest:

> Preparation programs aimed toward social justice are languishing in hypocrisy when faculty expect equity-oriented leaders to maintain high standards of accountability, supported by federal legislation, when these programs themselves engage in no systematic, empirical studies or equity audits of their own. Assessing leadership preparation should be the first priority in future research on preparing leaders for social justice (p. 219).

The call for this kind of leadership preparation could not be more timely, as many Western countries wrestle with demographic shifts and increasing diversity in schools.

Increased Allocation of Resources to Education

The resources allocated to education continue to come under attack in many countries, in some places like the USA, some are calling for the complete eradication of the Department of Education. In Ontario, under the former conservative government we have seen the devastating effects of cutbacks in education on the quality of education. This impacted the goal of bringing about greater equity in education as market forces take a greater hold on education systems around the world (Dei et al., 1999). Dei et al. argue that these reforms undermined public schooling and brought about an enormous blow to the future of antiracist and equity education in Ontario. Market-based education reforms do not place the struggles of marginalized youth high on the political agenda because many in society may not have any discomfort in seeing a predominantly White teaching body deliver education to minority and working-class populations (Delhi, 1994 as cited in Dei et al.; Solomon & Levine-Rasky, 1994).

The tides have shifted somewhat in Ontario with a Liberal government now in power that places greater focus on education, and articulates an equity perspective–Ontario Equity and Inclusive Strategy. This does not mean however that there is no more advocacy and equity work to be done. Those fighting for greater equity, culturally responsive and socially just education must keep their eye on the ball and be vigilant in fighting cutbacks that usually hurt students in communities with limited economic resources, racialized students, and students of color. Research has shown that the achievement gap can be reduced when resources are allocated that bring about greater equity in teaching and provide curriculum support. In the UK it was found that school-level spending on educational support and learning resources helped to close the achievement gap between advantaged and disadvantaged students (Nicoletti & Rabe, 2012).

How education is funded, and specifically amounts allocated to support equity initiatives, is intertwined with the policy discourse, and for that reason culturally responsive and socially just leaders cannot ignore how policy is formulated and implemented, and ways in which resources are allocated. Resource allocation is directly tied to the philosophies and ideologies of those in charge of funding education, and we have seen devastating results for programs that support marginalized youths when equity and social justice are not high on their agenda. Scholars and researchers have argued that neo-liberal policies that focus on efficiency and standardization have contributed to the gutting of resources allocated to education, and in some instances tied to outcomes that impact students and teachers negatively. Solomon et al. (2012) found in their research conducted with teachers in Ontario, Canada, that:

> …teachers have been increasingly marginalized from school budgetary decisions, a further indication of the bureaucratization of the profession… In fact, equity initiatives now require a great deal more paperwork than in the past… Some teachers wonder if administrators' concerns with budget cutbacks are a convenient excuse to discontinue any progressive work. In effect, most equity initiatives undertaken by teachers are and more in the hands of a top-down bureaucracy that discourages, rather than supports, social justice programs (p. 115).

Equity and social justice work on behalf of students cannot be done by will alone, and requires financial resources that can support programs and human resources to do the work. Cochran-Smith (2005) reminds educators that a focus on standards and accountability aligned to the high-stakes testing frenzy gripping education has the potential to sabotage the democratic goals of education. Neo-liberalism and the neo-liberal concept of choice have affected the education system greatly with the advancement of policies that have gutted public schools and seen the rise of charter schools and other for-profit schools often at the expense of public education and with funds that should have gone to supporting public education (Waite, Turan, & Nino, 2014). Waite et al. argue that "the continued erosion of public, governmental support for public education at all levels—preschool, primary, secondary, tertiary, vocational, and continuing adult education—suggest private, for-profit education as a more viable option" (p. 628). I support Waite et al. in their call to conscientious citizens to speak out against the gutting of public education that has been carried out in the name of efficiency and accountability.

Embedding Culturally Responsive and Socially Just Practices in Leadership, Teaching and Learning

If change is to occur in the lives of diverse and minoritized students, culturally responsive practices must be embedded in curriculum and leadership practices. Equity and social justice cannot be treated as an add-on. This requires training for teachers school leaders and administrators. Research is increasingly showing that school leaders, particularly school administrators, who implement culturally responsive and social practices support student achievement and improve teacher effectiveness (Branch et al., 2013). It is important that school administrators support teachers in this regard. Zeichner (2009) argues that the good intentions of teachers are not enough to address the crisis of inequality in public schools that denies poor children and children of color a high-quality education. One way of improving the education of diverse students is to make culturally relevant teaching and other equity approaches embedded in the curriculum and pedagogy (Lopez, 2013). I argue that it is important for teachers to dialogue with administrators about ways in which administration can support the work that they are doing in their classrooms. Embedding culturally responsive practices requires collaboration between the school administrators and teachers.

Many have argued that teacher education programs and principal training programs have a role to play in ensuring that teachers and principals are able to translate theory into action so that they can make change in their in their practice and schools. At the Ontario Institute for Studies in Education (OISE) University of Toronto, the former Bachelor of Education program made specific efforts to infuse equity and Aboriginal knowledge in the curriculum and the pedagogy of instructors who taught in the program. This was done through workshops and various curriculum supports. Efforts were also made to diversify the teacher education pool through initiatives such as Future Teachers Initiative, a program that I was the coordinator of from 2008–2011. The Future Teachers Initative focused specifically on encouraging students from marginalized communities to consider teaching as a career. It involved going to schools in areas with a large population of diverse and minority students and speaking with students about becoming teachers. A component of the Bachelor of Education program at OISE/UT was an Internship and each year approximately 12 teacher candidates completed their Internship in the Future Teachers Program. The teacher candidates who were involved in the program suggested that it was a very rewarding program for them.

Elsewhere in this book, I have talked about the importance of border crossing, not only for teachers and administrators from the dominant group, but also between diverse groups. Teacher education programs have a role to play in this regard. As Gay (2010) and others argue, culturally responsive training is important for teachers even when they are from the same cultural, racial, and socio-economic background. I have seen this need in my roles as a classroom teacher and school administrator working with educators from various racial and ethnic groups. Everyone benefits from a deeper understanding of ways to make culturally responsive practices the everyday norm. Khalifa et al. (2016) suggest that "the crucial role of the school leader is ensuring that teachers are and remain culturally responsive…the school leader [should] articulate a vision that supports the development and sustaining of culturally responsive teaching… she must have enough knowledge to recognize and challenge common patterns of inequities that lead to the disenfranchisement of poor urban youth" (p. 10). While I believe that school leaders must support teachers in their endeavors, I also argue that teachers must be encouraged to develop agency to act on their own behalf, even in instances when the school administrator might not be supportive. There is also the need for principal preparation programs to embed issues of equity and culturally responsive and socially just approaches in these programs. It is not enough for school leaders to learn on the job. While learning on the job has great value, is experiential, school administrators will benefit from having some understanding of the issues practically and theoretically before assuming their roles in schools. Jean-Marie, Normore, and Brooks (2009) suggest that the increasing diversity among leadership ranks calls for the provision of authentic and relevant experiences pertaining to leadership and social justice. They argue:

> Leadership preparation programs should promote opportunities for critical reflection, leadership praxis, critical discourse, and develop critical pedagogy related to issues of ethics, inclusion, democratic schooling, and social justice … efforts to increase the capacity of schools by broadening educators' work beyond conventional notions of teaching and administration would be improved by paying attention to how issues of social justice (e.g. gender, race, ethnicity, sexual orientation, etc.), shape and influence possibilities and desires for a more harmonious society that transcends national and international boundaries (p. 20).

Spring (2001) suggests that there is growing concern among educators that emerging school leaders are not well enough prepared to face the pressures that demographic shifts create in schools, and are therefore unable to advocate for an education that advances the rights and education of all children. Ensuring that culturally responsive and social justice approaches and practices are embedded in principal preparation programs requires a shift in the thinking around the development and delivery of those programs. Toure (2008) argues that those in educational leadership training should ensure that their programs have content that is culturally responsive and socially just.

It is my hope that as we think about and research and seek methodological clarity on issues that impact diverse learners, school leaders in all capacities will become engaged in that work. Structures within school systems that impede the progress of some students must be challenged and removed. This requires the work of school leaders who are not afraid to challenge the status quo. We must, however, recognize the tensions of the journey, what I call *tensions of practice* that school leaders face in these complex and changing times. It is my hope that some will find collaborative mentorship useful in supporting and sustaining them along their journey. The last chapter exposes my own vulnerabilities and journey in the hopes that others may learn from them. In this chapter I imagine a brighter future. It is important that school leaders and indeed all educators keep imagining a school system that is free of oppression where all students, no matter their background, can succeed. We must be hopeful and imagine possibilities as this lays the foundation for action. Imagining is important in the formation of self-identity within a community of practice. It is a way of looking at ourselves and our situations with new eyes, and being aware of multiple ways that we interpret our lives. As Dei et al. argue, the "task of transforming ... schools rests on conscious and sincere attempts to match the pursuit of academic excellence and quality education with considerations of equity and social justice. The promotion of excellence is inextricably linked with addressing access, equity and power issues in schools" (p. 9). When we imagine, we create possibilities for action and bringing what we imagine to reality. Imagining frees us from the constraints of an actual perceptual environment and places us into the realm of possibility. As educational leaders, when we begin to imagine a schooling system that is inclusive and values the knowledge and experiences of diverse learners, free from the hold of dominant ways of knowing, where the teaching and administrative staff reflect the diversity within its walls, we start the journey to making it a reality.

Those who advocate for social justice leadership and culturally responsive approaches believe that these frameworks offer workable theories that can guide the work of school leaders. While these theories undergird this book, I recognize the body of critical theories and research that have informed and continue to inform the understanding and practices of critical educators and school leaders (Banks, 2008; Giroux, 1992; Ladson-Billings, 1998; Sleeter, 2012). Educational leaders alone cannot bring about change in schools. It requires system-wide changes in polices and collaboration with teachers. Those who work in the area of policy must continue to do that work robustly as it often falls on the shoulders of teachers and school administrators to implement policy. Fowler (2013) defines public policy as "the dynamic and value-laden process through which a political system handles a public problem. It includes a government's expressed intentions and official enactments, as well as its consistent patterns of activity and inactivity" (p. 5). Education is governed by many policies that we know are political and value-laden, and hence critical educators must be vigilant in ensuring that educational policies are in the best interest of diverse learners and communities. As Khalifa et al. (2016) argue, as population demographics shift, so too must the leadership practices and school contexts that respond to the needs of students as these will make these practices meaningful and create lasting change. It is my hope that school leaders will embrace culturally responsive and socially just approaches that will ensure that all students will achieve and take their place in society, feeling empowered and excited about the future ahead.

Think Alouds—Questions for Reflection

1. How do you position your personal narratives as moments of teaching and learning?
2. In addtion to the areas highlghted as possible areas to focus on for the future, what areas would you add and why?
3. How might resource allocation be effectively distributed between competing demands and address issues of equity and diversity at the same time?
4. In what ways could principal training be improved to better prepare school leaders for diverse contexts?

Research Activity

1. How has your notion of leadership evolved? Besides culturally responsive leadership and social justice leadership which other leadership theories might be useful in undergirding your practice?
2. Drawing on your own experiences and leadership theories outline the possibilities that you imagine for the future

References

Achinstein, B. (2002). Conflict and community: The micropolitics of teacher collaboration. *Teachers College Press, 104*(3), 421–455.

Achinstein, B., & Athanases, S. (2005). Focusing new teachers on diversity and equity: Toward a knowledge base for mentors. *Teaching and Teacher Education, 21*, 843–862.

Adams, H. G. (1998). *The mentorship briefing guide: Handbook for establishing and implementing a program*. Notre Dame, IN: GEM Consortium.

Adams, H. G., & Scott, S. K. (1997). *The fundamentals of effective mentoring*. Notre Dame, IN: GEM Consortium.

Aguado, T., Ballesteros, B., & Malik, B. (2002). Cultural diversity and school equity: A model to evaluate and develop educational practices in multicultural contexts. *Equity and Excellence in Education, 35*, 50–61.

Allingham, N. (1992). *Anti-racism education and the curriculum: A privileged perspective in racism and education*. Ottawa, ON: Canadian Teachers Federation.

American Psychological Association, Presidential Task Force on Educational Disparities. (2012). *Ethnic and racial disparities in education: Psychology's contributions to understanding and reducing disparities*. Retrieved from http://www.apa.org/ed/resources/racial-disparities.aspx

Anderson, A. R., Christenson, S. L., Sinclair, M. F., & Lehr, C. A. (2004). Check & connect: The importance of relationships for promoting engagement with school. *Journal of School Psychology, 42*(2), 95–113.

Anderson, E. M., & Shannon, A. L. (1988). Toward a conceptualization of mentoring. *Journal of Teacher Education, 39*(1), 38–42.

Anthias, F., & Yuval-Davis, N. (1993). *Racialized boundaries, race, nation, gender, color and class and the anti-racist struggle*. New York, NY: Routledge Press.

A.E. Lopez, *Culturally Responsive and Socially Just Leadership in Diverse Contexts*, DOI 10.1057/978-1-137-53339-5

Appleton, C. (2011). 'Critical friends' feminism and integrity: A reflection on the use of critical friends as a research tool to support research, integrity and reflexivity in qualitative research studies. *Women in Welfare Education Collective*, 10. Retrieved from http://www.freepatentsonline.com/article/women-in-welfare-Education/299639543.html

Appleton, J. J., Christenson, S. L., & Furlong, M. J. (2008). Student engagement with school: Critical conceptual and methodological issues of the construct. *Psychology in Schools, 45*, 369–386.

Argyris, C., & Schon, D. A. (1996). *Organizational learning 11: Theory, method and practice*. Reading, MA: Addison-Wesley.

Armstrong, D., Tuters, S., & Carrier, N. (2013). Micropolitics and social justice leadership: Bridging beliefs and behaviors. *Journal of Educational Administration and Foundation, 23*(2), 119–137.

Aylward, C. (2000). *Canadian critical race theory: Racism and the law*. Halifax: Fernwood Publishing.

Bajaj, M. (2015). 'Pedagogies of resistance' and critical peace education praxis. *Journal of Peace Education, 12*(2), 154–166. doi:10-1080/17400201120l4.9991914.

Ball, A. F., & Tyson, C. T. (2011). *Studying diversity in teacher education*. Lanham, MD: Rowman & Littlefield Publishers Inc. in Partnership with the American Educational Research Association.

Ball, S. J. (1987). *The micro-politics of the school. Towards a theory of school organization*. London: Routledge.

Bamberg, M. (2011). Who am I? Narration and its contributions to self and identity. *Theory & Psychology, 21*(1), 3–24.

Banks, C. (2005). *Improving multicultural education: Lessons from the intergroup education movement*. New York: Teachers College Press.

Banks, C. M., & Banks, J. A. (1995). Equity pedagogy: An essential component of multicultural education. *Theory Into Practice, 34*(3), 152–158.

Banks, J. A. (2007). *Educating citizens in a multicultural society* (2nd ed.). New York: Teachers College Press.

Banks, J. A. (2008). Diversity, group identity, and citizenship education in a global age. *Educational Researcher, 37*(3), 129–139.

Banks, J. A. (2009). Diversity and citizenship education in multicultural nations. *Multicultural Education Review, 1*(1), 1–28.

Bates, R. (2001). Can we manage global education? Paper presented to the *Annual Conference of the Canadian Society for the Study of Educational Administration*. University of Laval, Quebec City, May 23–26, 2001.

Baxter Magolda, M. B. (2001). *Making their own way: Narratives for transforming higher education to promote self-development*. Sterling, VA: Stylus.

Beachum, F. (2011). Culturally relevant leadership for complex 21st century school contexts. In F. English (Ed.), *The Sage handbook of educational leadership* (4th ed., pp. 27–35). Thousand Oaks, CA: Sage Publications.

Beachum, F., & McCray, C. (2004). Cultural collision in urban schools. *Current Issues in Education, 7*(5), 1–5. Retrieved from http://cie.asu.edu/ojs/index.php/cieatsu/article/view/821/247

Berry, A. (2008). *Tensions in teaching about teaching: Understanding practice as a teacher educator.* Dordrecht, The Netherlands: Springer.

Bingham, G. E., & Okagaki, L. (2012). Ethnicity and student engagement. In A. Christenson, A. Reschly, & C. Wylie (Eds.), *Handbook of research on student engagement* (pp. 65–95). New York, NY: Springer.

Bjork, L. G., & Blase, J. (2009). The micropolitics of school district decentralization. *Educational Assessment, Evaluation and Accountability, 21*(3), 195–208.

Blackmore, J. (2009). Leadership for social justice: A transnational dialogue. *Journal of Research on Leadership in Education, 4*(1), 1–10.

Blankstein, A. M., & Noguera, P. (2015). Achieving excellence through equity for every student. In A. Blankstein & P. Noguera (Eds.), *Excellence through equity* (pp. 3–30). Thousand Oaks, CA: Sage Publications.

Blase, J. (1991). Everyday political perspectives of teachers toward students: The dynamics of diplomacy. In J. Blase (Ed.), *The politics of schools: Power, conflict and cooperation.* Newbury, CA: Sage.

Blase, J. (1993). The micropolitics of effective school-based leadership: Teachers' perspectives. *Educational Administration Quarterly, 29*(2), 142–163.

Bogotch, I. E. (2002). Leadership for socially just schooling: More substance and less style in high-risk, low-trust times. *Journal of School Leadership, 12*(2), 198–222.

Bogotch, I. E. (2005). *Social justice as an educational construct: Problems and possibilities.* Paper presented at the annual meeting of the University Council of Educational Administration, Nashville, TN, November.

Bogotch, I. E. (2014). Educational theory: The specific case of social justice as an educational leadership construct. In I. Bogotch & C. Shield (Eds.), *International handbook of educational leadership and social (in)justice* (pp. 51–66). New York, NY: Springer.

Bogotch, I., & Reyes-Guerra, D. (2014). Leadership for social justice: Social pedagogies. *Revista Internacional de Educacion para la Justicia Social, 3*(2), 33–58.

Bogotch, I., & Shields, C. (Eds.). (2014). Introduction: Do promises of social justice trump paradigms of educational leadership? In *International handbook of educational leadership and social (in)justice* (pp. 1–14). New York, NY: Springer.

Bondy, E., Ross, D. D., Gallingane, C., & Hambacher, E. (2007). Culturally responsive classroom management and more: Creating environments of success and resilience. *Urban Education, 42*(4), 326–348.

Borofsky, R., Barth, F., Shweda, R., Rodseth, L., & Stolzenberg, R. (2001). When a conversation about culture. *American Anthropologist, 103*, 432–446.

Branch, G., Hanushek, E., & Rivkin, S. (2013). School leaders matter. *Education Next, 13*(1), 62–69. Retrieved from http://educationnext.org/school-leaders-matter/

Brayboy, B. (2005). Transformational resistance and social justice: American Indians in ivy league universities. *Anthropology and Education Quarterly, 36*(3), 191–211.

Britzman, D. (1998). *Lost subjects, contested objects: Toward a psychoanalytic inquiry of learning*. Albany, NY: State University of New York Press.

Britzman, D. (2003). *Practice makes practice: A critical study of learning to teach*. Albany, NY: State University of New York Press.

Brooks, J. S. (2012). Educational leadership and social justice: Patterns to the present, possibilities for the future and future. In E. Murakami-Ramalho & A. Pankake (Eds.), *Educational leaders encouraging the intellectual and professional capacity of others* (pp. xi–xiii). Charlotte, NC: Information Age Publishing.

Brooks, J., Normore, A., & Jean-Marie, G. (Eds.). (2014). Educational leadership and conflict in international contexts. *Planning and Changing*, 44(3/4).

Brown, F. (2005). African Americans and school leadership: An introduction. *Educational Administration Quarterly, 41*(4), 585–590.

Bullough, R. V., & Pinnegar, S. (2001). Guidelines for quality in autobiographical forms of self-study research. *Educational Researcher, 30*(3), 13–21.

Capper, C. A., Theoharis, G., & Sebastian, J. (2006). Toward a framework for preparing leaders for social justice. *Journal of Educational Administration, 44*(3), 209–224. doi:10.1108/09578230610664814.

Carspecken, P. (1996). *Critical ethnography in educational research: A theoretical and practical guide*. New York: NY Routledge.

Casella, R. (2003). Zero tolerance policy in schools: Rationale, consequences and alternatives. *Teachers College Record, 105*, 872–892.

Castle, J., & Mitchell, L. (2001). *Roles of elementary school principals in Ontario: Tasks and tensions – An executive summary*. Brock, St. Catharines: ON Faculty of Education, Brock University.

Cho, H. (2011). Lessons learned: Teaching the race concept in the college classroom. *Multicultural Perspectives, 13*(1), 36–41.

Chou, C. C. (2008). Critique on the notion of model minority: An alternative racism to Asian American. *Asian Ethnicity, 9*(3), 219–229.

Clandinin, D. J., & Connelly, F. M. (2000). *Narrative inquiry: Experience and story in qualitative research*. San Francisco, CA: Jossey-Bass.

Clarke, M. C., Koch, L. L., & Hill, E. J. (2004). The work-family interface: Differentially balance and fit. *Family and Consumer Sciences Research Journal, 33*(2), 121–140.

Cleary, T. J., & Zimmerman, B. J. (2012). A cyclical self-regulation account of student engagement: Theoretical foundations and applications. In A. Christenson, A. Reschly, & C. Wylie (Eds.), *Handbook of research on student engagement* (pp. 237–257). New York, NY: Springer.

Cochran-Smith, M. (2003a). Learning and unlearning: The education of teacher educators. *Teaching and Teacher Education, 19*, 5–28.

Cochran-Smith, M. (2003b). The multiple meanings of multicultural teacher education: A conceptual framework. *Teacher Education Quarterly, 30*(20), 7–26.

Cochran-Smith, M. (2005). Teacher education and the outcomes trap. *Journal of Teacher Education, 56*(5), 411–417.

Cochran-Smith, M., Davis, D., & Fries, K. (2004). Multicultural teacher education: Research, practice, and policy. In J. Banks & C. Banks (Eds.), *Handbook of research on multicultural education* (2nd ed., pp. 931–975). New York, NY: Macmillan.

Cochran-Smith, M., & Lytle, S. (2009). *Inquiry as stance: Practitioner research for the next generation.* New York, NY: Teachers College Press.

Cohen, N. H. (2002). The journey of the principles of adult mentoring inventory. *Adult Learning, 14*(1), 4–7.

Cole, B. P. (1986). The black educator: An endangered species. *Journal of Negro Education, 55*(3), 326–334.

Cooper, R., & Jordan, W. J. (2003). Cultural issues in comprehensive school reform. *Urban Education, 38*(4), 380–397.

Covell, K., McNeil, J., & Howe, R. B. (2009). Reducing teacher burnout by increasing student engagement: A children's rights approach. *School Psychology International, 30*(3), 282–290.

Cross, S. W., Parham, T. A., & Helms, J. E. (1991). Nigresene revisited. Theory and research. In R. L. Jones (Ed.), *Advances in Black psychology* (3rd ed., pp. 319–338). Berkley, CA: Cobb & Henry.

Cross, W. E. (1991). *Shades of Black: Diversity in African American identity.* Philadephia, PA: Temple University Press.

Cushman, K., & Rogers, L. (2008). *Fires in the middle school bathroom: Advice for teachers from middle schoolers.* New York, NY: The New Press.

Daniel, Y., & Bondy, K. (2008). Safe schools and zero tolerance: Policy, program and practice in Ontario. *Canadian Journal of Educational Administration and Policy*, Iuuse # 70, February 28.

Dantley, M. (1990). The ineffectiveness of effective schools leadership: An analysis of the effective schools movement from a critical perspective. *Journal of Negro Education, 59*(4), 585–598.

Dantley, M. E., & Tillman, L. C. (2010). Social justice and moral transformative leadership. In C. Marshall & M. Olivia (Eds.), *Leadership for social justice* (2nd ed., pp. 19–34). Boston, MA: Allyn & Bacon.

Daresh, J. (2004). Mentoring school leaders: Professional promise or predictable problems? *Educational Administration Quarterly, 40*(4), 495–517.

Darling-Hammond, L. (1997). *Doing what matters most: Investing in quality teaching.* Kutztown, PA: National Commission on Teaching and America's Future.

Darling-Hammond, L. (2003). Kepping good teachers: Why it matters what leaders can do. *Educational Leadership, 60*(8), 6–13.

Darling-Hammond, L. (2011). Foreword. In A. Ball & C. Tyson (Eds.), *Studying diversity in teacher education* (pp. ix–ix). Lanham, MD: Rowman & Littlefield.

David, D. J. (2008). The mentorship of a sharecropper's daughter: Being young, gifted, and black in academe. In C. A. Mullen (Ed.), *The handbook of formal mentoring in higher education: A case study approach* (pp. 78–83). Norwood, MA: Christopher-Gordon.

Davis, D. M. (2002). Toward democratic education: The importance of culturally responsive leadership in 21st century schools. *Trotter Review, 14*(1). Retrieved from http://scholarworks.umb.edu/trotter_Review/vol14/ss/1/3/

Davis, S., Darling-Hammond, L., LaPointe, M., & Meyerson, D. (2005). *Developing successful principals.* Stanford, CA: Stanford Educational Leadership Institute.

Day, C., Harris, A., & Hadfield, M. (2001). Challenging the orthodox of effective a=school leadership. *International Journal of Leadership in Education, 4*(1), 39–56.

Dee, T. S. (2005). A teacher like me: Does race, ethnicity, or gender matter? *American Economic Review, 95*(2), 158–165.

Dehli, K. (1994). *Parent activism and school reform in Toronto.* Toronto, ON: Report to the Ontario Ministry of Education and Training.

Dehli, K. (1996). Between "market" and "state"? Engendering education change in the 1990s. *Discourse: Studies in The Cultural Politics of Education, 17*(3), 363–376.

Dei, G. J. S. (1999). Aurora interview Mike Gismondi. Retrieved from http://www.aurora/icaap.org/talks/dei/html

Dei, G. J. S. (2000). Towards an anti-racism discursive framework. In G. J. S. Dei & A. Calliste (Eds.), *Power, knowledge and anti-racism education* (pp. 23–40). Halifax, NS: Fernwood Publishing.

Dei, G. J. S. (2008). Crash and the relevance of an anti-racism analytical lens. In P. Howard & G. J. S. Dei (Eds.), *Crash politics and antiracism-interrogations of liberal race discourse* (pp. 13–24). New York, NY: Peter Lang Publishing.

Dei, G. J. S. (2015). Reflections on dropping out of school: Meeting the challenge of youth engagement. Retrieved from http://www.cea-ace.ca/eduation-canada/article/reflections-"dropping-out"-school

Dei, G. J. S., & Doyle-wood, S. (2009). Is wo whohaffi ride di stamm: Critical knowledge/multiple knowings—Possibilities, challenges, and resistance in curriculum/cultural studies. In Y. Kanu (Ed.), *Curriculum as cultural practice: Postcolonial imaginations* (pp. 151–180). Toronto, ON: University of Toronto Press.

Dei, G. J. S., James, I. M., Karumanchery, L. L., James-Wilson, S., & Zine, J. (2000). *Removing the margins: The challenges and possibilities of inclusive schooling.* Toronto, ON: Canadian Scholars' Press Inc..

Dei, G. J. S., Karumanchery, J., & Leeno, L. (1999). School reforms in Ontario: The marketization of education and the resulting silence on equity. *Alberta Journal of Education, 45*(2), 111–131.

Dei, G. J. S., Mazzuca, J., McIsaac, E., & Zine, J. (1997). *Reconstructing "drop-out": A critical ethnography of the dynamics of black students' disengagement from school* (pp. 3–30, 46–84). Toronto, ON: University of Toronto Press.

Denzin, N. K., & Lincoln, Y. S. (2005). *The Sage handbook of qualitative research* (3rd ed.). Thousand Oaks, CA: Sage Publications.

Dewey, J. (1938). *Experience and education.* London: Colter-Macmillan.

Dewey, J. (1964). *Democracy and education.* New York: Free Press.

DiAngelo, R. (2011). White fragility. *International Journal of Critical Pedagogy, 3*(3), 54–70.

DiPaola, M., Tarter, C., & Hoy, W. K. (2005). School characteristics that foster organizational citizenship behavior. *Journal of School Leadership, 15*(4), 387–406.

Dunleavy, J., & Milton, P. (2009). *What did you do in school today? Exploring the concept of student engagement and its implications for teaching and learning in Canada* (pp. 1–22). Toronto, ON: Canadian Education Association.

Dunleavy, J., Milton, P., & Crawford, C. (2010). The search for competence in the 21st century. *Quest Journal 2010.* Leading Edge Learning. Retrieved from http://www.leadingedgelearning.ca/q2010/Docs/QuestJournal/2010/Article12.pdf

Durham-Barnes, J. (2011). The balancing act: The personal and professional challenges of urban teachers. *Perspectives on Urban Education, 9*(11), 1–11.

Durrant, J., & Holden, G. (2006). *Teachers leading change.* London: Paul Chapman.

Eccles, J. S., Wigfield, A., & Schiefele, U. (1998). Motivation. In N. Eisenberg (Ed.), *Handbook of child psychology* (pp. 1017–1095). New York, NY: Wiley.

Edmunds, B., Mulford, B., Kendall, D., & Kendall, L. (2008). Leadership tensions and dilemmas. *International Electronic Journal for Leadership in Learning, 12*(1), 1–17.

Equity and Excellence Commission. (2013). *For each and every child: A strategy for education equity and excellence.* Washington, DC. Retrieved from http://www.foreachandeverychild.org/The_Report.html

Evans, A. E. (2007). Horton, highlander, and leadership education: Lessons for preparing educational leaders for social justice. *Journal of School Leadership, 17*(3), 250–275.

Feldman, S. B., & Tyson, K. (2014). Clarifying conceptual foundations for social justice in education. In *International handbook of educational leadership and social (in)justice* (pp. 1105–1124). Dordrecht, NL: Springer doi:10.1007/978-94-007-6555-9_55

Finn, J. (1989). Withdrawing from school. *Review of Educational Research, 59*(2), 117–142.

Finn, J. D., & Rock, D. A. (1997). Academic success among student at risk for school failure. *Journal of Applied Psychology, 82*(20), 1221–1324.

Forde, C. (2014). Issues of social justice and fairness in the development of aspiring head teachers: I had not really thought about my values before. In I. Bogotch & C. Shields (Eds.), *International handbook of educational leadership and social (in)justice* (pp. 1125–1144). Dordrecht, NL: Springer.

Foster, W. F. (1986). *The reconstruction of leadership*. Victoria, Australia: Deakin University Press.

Foster, W. F. (1989). Towards a critical practice of leadership. In J. Smyth (Ed.), *Critical prospectus on educational leadership*. London: The Falmer Press.

Fowler, F. C. (2013). *Policy studies for educational leaders: An introduction* (4th ed.). Upper Saddle River, NJ: Pearson.

Fraise, N. J., & Brooks, J. S. (2015). Toward a theory of culturally relevant leadership for school-community culture. *International Journal of Multicultural Education, 17*(1), 6–21. Retrieved from http://ijme-journal.org/index.php/ijme/article/view/983/1042

Fredericks, J., Blumenfeld, P. C., & Paris, A. (2004). School engagement: Potential of the concept: State of the evidence. *Review of Educational Research, 74*(1), 59-109.

Fredricks, J. A., & McColskey, W. (2012). The measurement of student engagement: A comparative analysis of various methods and student self-report instruments. In S. L. Christenson, A. L. Reschly, & C. Wylie (Eds.), *The handbook of research on student engagement* (pp. 763–782). New York, NY: Springer Science.

Freire, P. (1970). *Pedagogy of the oppressed*. New York, NY: Herder and Herder.

Freire, P. (1998). *Politics and education*. Los Angeles, CA: ULCA Latin American Center Publications.

Frost, D. (2006). The concept of 'agency' in leadership for learning. *Leading and Managing, 12*(2), 19–28.

Fullan, M. (2003). *The moral imperative of school leadership*. Thousand Oaks, CA: Corwin Press; Toronto, ON: Ontario Principals' Council.

Fullan, M. (2005). *Leadership & sustainability: Systems thinkers in action*. Thousand Oaks, CA: Corwin Press.

Fullan, M. (2014). *The principal: Three keys to maximizing impact*. San Francisco, CA: Jossey-Bass.

Furman, G. (2012). Social justice leadership as praxis: Developing capacities through preparation programs. *Educational Administration Quarterly, 48*(2), 191–229.

Gay, G. (2000). *Culturally responsive teaching: Theory, research, and practice*. New York, NY: Teachers College Press.

Gay, G. (2010a). Acting on beliefs in teacher education for cultural diversity. *Journal of Teacher Education, 61*(1–2), 143–152.

Gay, G. (2010b). *Culturally responsive teaching: Theory, research, and practice* (2nd ed.). New York, NY: Teachers College Press.

Gayle, B. M., Cortez, D., & Preiss, R. W. (2013). Safe spaces, different dialogue, and critical thinking. *International Journal of Scholarship of Teaching and Learning, 7*(2), Article 5. doi:10.20429/ijostl.2013.070205

Giroux, H. A. (1992). *Border crossing: Cultural workers and the politics of education.* New York, NY: Routledge.

Gonzalez, N., Moll, L., & Amanti, C. (2005). *Funds of knowledge: Theorizing practices in households, communities and classrooms.* Mahwah, NJ: Lawrence Erlbaum Associates.

Goodard, Y. L., Neumerski, L., Goddard, R. D., Salloum, S., & Berebitsking, D. (2010). A multilevel exploratory study of the relationship between teachers' perceptions of principals instructional support and group norms for instruction in elementary schools. *Elementary School Journal, 11*(2), 336–357.

Gooden, M. A. (2005). The role of an African American principal in an urban information technology high school. *Educational Administration Quarterly, 41*(4), 630–650. doi:10.1177/0013161X04274273.

Gooden, M. A., & Dantley, M. (2012). Centering race in a framework for leadership preparation. *Journal of Research on Leadership Education, 7*, 237–253. doi: 10.1177/1o42775112455266.

Gordon, J. A. (2000). *The color of teaching.* New York, NY: Rutledge Farmer.

Grant, C. A., & Sleeter, C. E. (2011). *Doing multicultural education for achievement and equity* (2nd ed.). New York, NY: Routledge.

Green, M. J. (2014). On the inside looking in methodological insights and challenges in conducting qualitative insider research. *The Qualitative Report 19*(29), 1–13. Retrieved from http://www.nova.edu/SSSS/QR/QR19/greene15.pdf

Greene, B. A., Miller, R. B., Crowson, H. M., Duke, B. L., & Akey, A. L. (2004). Predicting high school students' cognitive engagement and achievement: Contributions of classroom perceptions and motivation. *Contemporary Educational Psychology, 29*(4), 462–482.

Grossman, H. (1995). *Teaching in a diverse society.* Needham Heights, MA: Allyn & Bacon.

Gunter, H. M. (2006). Educational leadership and the challenge of diversity. *Educational Management Administration Leadership, 34*(2), 257–268.

Ham, L. D., & Cormier, K. J. (2015). *School leaders face complex racial issues in diverse schools and communities.* Montreal, QC: McGill-Queen's University Press. Retrieved from https://journals.lib.unb.ca/index.php/antistasis/article/download/22861/26621

Hargreaves, A., & Fullan, M. (1998). *What's worth fighting for out there.* New York, NY: Teachers College Press.

Harper, S. R. (2013). *Five things student affairs administrators can do to improve success amongst college men of color*. Washington, DC: NASPA Research and Policy Institute Issue Brief.

Harper, S. R., Berhanu, J., Davis, C. F., & McGuire, K. M. (2015). Engaging college men of color. In S. J. Quaye & S. R. Harper (Eds.), *Student engagement in higher education: Theoretical perspectives and practical approaches for diverse populations*. New York, NY: Routledge.

Harper, S. R., & Quaye, S. J. (2015). Making engagement equitable for students in U.S. higher education. In S. J. Quaye & S. R. Harper (Eds.), *Student engagement in higher education: Theoretical perspectives and practical approaches for diverse populations* (2nd ed., pp. 1–20). New York, NY: Routledge.

Harrell, J. P., Hall, S., & Taliaferro, J. (2003). Physiological responses to racism and discrimination: An assessment of the evidence. *American Journal of Public Health, 93*(3), 243–248.

Harris, R. (2008). A phenomenographic investigation of teacher conceptions of student engagement in learning. *The Australian Educational Researcher, 5*(1), 57–79.

Heddy, B. B., & Sinatra, G. M. (2013). Transforming misconceptions: Using transformative experience to promote positive affect and conceptual change in students learning about biological evolution. *Science Education, 97*(5), 725–744. doi:10!1002/sce.21072.

Henry, F., & Tator, C. (Eds.). (2009). *Racism in the Canadian university: Demanding social justice, inclusion, and equity*. Toronto, ON: University of Toronto Press.

Hinchey, P. (2008). *Becoming a critical educator: Defining a classroom identity, designing a critical pedagogy*. New York, NY: Peter Lang.

Hoffman, J. (2005). *Violence at school: Can hard-line policies top school violence- or do they ignore the real problem?* Retrieved from http://www.todaysparent.com

Holloway, J. (2002). The dilemma of zero tolerance. *Educational Leadership, 59*(4), 84–86.

Holloway, J. (2004). Leading in tough times. *Educational Leadership, 61*(7), 87–88.

Horsford, S. D. (2010). *New perspectives in political as leadership: Exploring social political, and community contexts and meaning*. New York, NY: Peter Lang.

Howard, G. R. (2007). As diversity grows, so must we. *Educational Leadership, 64*(6), 16–22.

Howard, T. C. (2003). The dis(g)race of the social studies: The need for racial dialogue in the social studies. In G. Ladson-Billings (Ed.), *Critical race theory on social studies: The profession policies and curriculum* (pp. 27–43). New York, NY: Information Age Publishing.

Irvine, J. J. (1988). An analysis of the problem of the disappearing Black educators. *The Elementary School Journal, 88*(5), 503–514.

Irvine, JJ., & McAllister, G. (2000). Cross cultural competency and multicultural teacher education. *Review of Educational Research, 70*(1), 3–24.

James, C. E., & Brathwaite, K. S. (1996). The education of African Canadians: Issues, contexts, and expectations. In K. S. Brathwaite & C. E. James (Eds.), *Educating African Canadians* (pp. 13–31). Toronto, ON: James Lormier.

Janans, M. (1996). Mentoring the mentor: A challenge for staff development. *Journal of Staff Development, 17*(4), 2–5.

Jean-Marie, G. (2008). Leadership for social justice: An agenda for 21st century schools. *The Educational Forum, 72*(4), 340–354.

Jean-Marie, G., & Normore, A. H. (Eds.). (2010). *Educational leadership preparation: Innovation and interdisciplinary approaches to the Ed.D. and graduate education*. New York, NY: Palgrave Macmillan.

Jean-Marie, G., Normore, A. H., & Brooks, J. S. (2009). Leadership for social justice: Preparing 21st century school leaders for a new social order. *Journal of Research on Leadership, 4*(1), 1–31.

Jehangir, R. R. (2012). Conflict as catalyst for learning. *About Campus, 17*(2), 2–8.

Jelinek, E. (1986). *The tradition of women's autobiography: From antiquity to the present*. Boston, MA: G.K. Hall.

Johnson, L. (2014). Culturally responsive leadership for community empowerment. *Multicultural Education Review, 6*(2), 145–170.

Kea, C. D., Trent, S. C., & Davis, C. P. (2002). African American student teachers perceptions about preparedness to teach students from culturally and linguistically diverse backgrounds. *Multicultural Perspectives, 4*(1), 18–25.

Kezar, A., Walpole, M., & Perna, L. (2014). Engaging low-income students. In S. J. Quaye & S. R. Harper (Eds.), *Student engagement in higher education: Theoretical perspectives and practical approaches for diverse populations* (pp. 237–257). New York, NY: Routledge.

Khalifa, M. (2013). Creating spaces for urban youth: The emergence of culturally responsive (hip-hop) school leadership and pedagogy. *Multicultural Learning and Teaching, 8*(2), 63–93. doi:10.1515/mlt-2013-0010.

Khalifa, M., Gooden, M., & Davis, J. (2016). Culturally responsive school leadership: A synthesis of the literature. *Review of Educational Research, 0034654316630383, first published on February 12, 2016 as doi:10.3102/0034654316630383*, 1–40.

Kimbrough, W. M., & Harper, S. R. (2006). African-American men at historically Black colleges and universities: Different environments, similar challenges. In M. J. Cuyjet (Ed.), *African-American men in college* (pp. 189–209). San Francisco, CA: Jossey-Bass.

Kincheloe, J. L., & McLaren, P. L. (2008). Rethinking critical theory and qualitative research. In N. K. Denzin & Y. S. Lincoln (Eds.), *The landscape of qualitative research: Theories and issues* (pp. 260–299). Thousand Oaks, CA: Sage Publications.

Knapp, M. S., Copland, M., & Talbert, J. E. (2003). *Leading for learning: Reflective tools for school and district leaders*. Seattle, WA: University of Washington Center for the Study of Teaching and Policy.

Knoepfel, P., Larrue, C., Varnone, F., & Hill, M. (2007). *Public policy analysis.* Bristol, U.K.: The Policy Press.

Koki, S. (2011). *The role of teacher mentoring in educational reform.* Retrieved from http://bdgrdemocracy.files.wordpress.com

Kovalenko, S. (2012). *Ontario Safe Schools Act and its effects on racialized immigrant youth: School to prison pipeline.* Theses and dissertations. Paper 1544. Retrieved from http://digitalcommons.ryerson.ca/dissertaion

Ladson-Billings, G. (1995a). But that's just good teaching! The case for culturally relevant pedagogy. *Theory Into Practice, 34*(3), 159–165.

Ladson-Billings, G. J. (1995b). Toward a critical race theory of education. *Teachers College Record, 97*(1), 47–68.

Ladson-Billings, G. J. (1995c). Toward a theory of culturally relevant pedagogy. *American Education Research Journal, 32*(3), 465–491.

Ladson-Billings, G. (1998). Just what is critical race theory and what's it doing in a nice field like education? *International Journal of Qualitative Studies in Education, 11*(1), 7–24. doi:10.1080/095183998236863.

Ladson-Billings, G. (2000). Racialized discourses and ethnic epistemologies. In N. Denzin & Y. Lincoln (Eds.), *Handbook of qualitative research* (2nd ed.). Thousand Oaks, CA: Sage.

Ladson-Billings, G. (2014). Culturally relevant pedagogy 2.0 a.k.a. the remix. *Harvard Educational Review, 84*(1), 74–84.

Lee, E. (2009). Taking multicultural, anti-racist education seriously: An interview with Enid Lee. In W. Au (Ed.), *Rethinking multicultural education: Teaching for racial and cultural justice* (pp. 9–16). Milwaukee, WI: Rethinking Schools.

Leithwood, K., & Jantzi, D. (2006). Transformational leadership for large-scale reform: Effects on students, teachers, and their classroom practices. *School Effectiveness and School Improvement, 17*(2), 201–227. doi:10.1080/09243450600565829.

Leithwood, K., Seashore-Louis, K. S., Anderson, S., & Wahlstrom, K. (2004). *How leadership influences student learning: Review of research.* New York, NY: Wallace Foundation.

Leo, E. L., & Barton, L. (2006). Inclusion, diversity and leadership: Perspectives, possibilities and contradictions. *Educational Management Administration and Leadership, 34*(2), 167–176.

Lewison, M., Leland, C., & Harste, J. C. (2007). *Creating critical classrooms: Reading and writing with an edge.* Mahwah, NJ: Lawrence Erlbaum.

Linnenbrink-Garcia, L., & Pekrun, R. (2011). Students' emotions and academic engagement: Introduction to the special issue. *Contemporary Educational Psychology, 36*(1), 1–3.

Lipton, L., & Wellman, B. (2003). *Mentoring matters: A practical guide to learning focused relationships.* Sherman, CT: Mira via, LLC.

Lopez, A. E. (2005). *Implementing integrative anti-racist education: Negotiating conflicts and tensions utilizing experiential collaborative mentorship.* Unpublished doctoral dissertation, University of Toronto.

Lopez, A. (2006). *Making it real: Problematizing the curriculum, opening up critical spaces for students.* Paper presented at the Canadian Society for Studies in Education (CSSE), York University, Toronto.

Lopez, A. E. (2011). Culturally relevant pedagogy and critical literacy in diverse English classrooms: Case study of a secondary English teacher's activism and agency. *English Teaching Practice and Critique, 10*(4), 75–93.

Lopez, A. E. (2013). Embedding and sustaining equitable practices in teachers' everyday work: A framework for critical action. *Teaching & Learning, 7*(3), 1–15.

Lopez, A. E. (2014). Re-conceptualizing teacher leadership through curriculum inquiry in pursuit of social justice: Case study from the Canadian context. In C. Shields & I. Bogotch (Eds.), *International handbook of educational leadership and social (in)justice* (pp. 465–484). Dordrecht, NL: Springer.

Lopez, A. E. (2015). Navigating cultural borders in diverse contexts: Building capacity through culturally responsive leadership and critical praxis. *Multicultural Education Review, 7*(3), 171–184.

Lopez, A. E. (2016a). *Dauntless and determined: Reimagining culturally responsive leadership on current contexts, changing times and shifting landscapes.* Paper presented at AERA, Washington, DC, April.

Lopez, A. E. (2016b). Voices from the field: What can we learn from school leaders in diverse schools? Possibilities and tensions. In S. Choo, D. Sawch, A. Villanueva, & R. Vinz (Eds.), *Educating for the 21st century: Perspectives, policies and practices from around the world* (pp. 117-129). Singapore: Springer.

Lopez, A.E. & Olan, E. (Forthcoming). Critical practices for teaching and learning in global contexts,: Building bridges for action. In R. Shin (Ed.), *Contemporary art, visual culture, and global civic engagement Hershey*, PA: IGI Global.

Lyman, L. L., & Villani, C. J. (2002). The complexity of poverty: A missing component of educational leadership programs. *Journal of School Leadership, 12*(3), 246–280.

Madhlangobe, L., & Gordon, S. P. (2012). Culturally responsive leadership in a diverse school: A case study of a high school leader. *NASSP Bulletin, 96*(3), 177–202. doi:10.1177/0192636512450909.

Marshall, C. (2004). Social justice challenges to educational administration: Introduction to a special issue. *Educational Administration Quarterly, 40*(1), 3–13.

Mascuch, M. (1997). *The origins of the individualist self: Autobiography and self-identity in England 1591-1791.* London: Wiley.

Maxwell, K. (2014). *Evaluating the effectiveness of two teaching strategies to improve nursing students' knowledge, skills, and attitudes in quality improvement and patient safety.* PhD dissertation. Retrieved from http://acunen.lb.ua.edu/Content/u0015/000000/0001640/00015_000001_000164.pdf

Mayo, C. (2002). The binds tht tie: Civility and social difference. *Education Theory, 52*(2), 169–186.

McKenzie, K. B., Christman, D. E., Hernandez, F., Fierro, E., Capper, C. A., Dantley, M., et al. (2008). From the field: A proposal for educating leaders for social justice. *Educational Administration Quarterly, 44*(1), 111–138.

McLaren, P. (1995). *Critical pedagogy and predatory culture: Oppositional policies in a postmodern era.* New York: Routledge.

McLaren, P. (1998). *Life in schools: An introduction to critical pedagogy in foundations to education.* New York: Longman.

McMahon, B., Munns, G., Smyth, J., & Zyngires, D. (2012). Student engagement for equity and social justice: Creating space for student voice. *Teaching and Learning, 7*(2), 63–78.

McMahon, B., & Portelli, J. P. (2004). Engagement for what? Beyond popular discourses of student engagement. *Leadership and Policy in Schools, 3*(1), 59–76.

Miles, R. (1989). *Racism.* London: Routledge.

Miller, P. C., & Endo, H. (2005). Journey to becoming a teacher: The experiences of students of color. *Multicultural Education, 13*(1), 2–9.

Montano, T., Lopez-Torres, L., DeLissovoy, N., Pacheo, M., & Stillman, J. (2002). Teachers as activists: Teacher development and alternate sites of learning. *Equity and Excellence in Education, 35*(3), 265–275.

Mosher, J.E. (2008). Lessons to access in justice: Racialized youths in Ontario's safe schools. *Osgoode Hall Law Journal, 70*(1), 3–24 Retrieved from http://digitalcommons.osgoodeyourku.ca

Mulford, B. (2003a). *School leaders: Changing roles and impact on teacher and school effectiveness.* Commissioned paper by the Education and Training Policy Division, OECD, for the activity "Attracting, Developing and Retaining Effective Teachers". Paris: OECD. Retrieved from http://www.oecd.org/dataoecd/61/61/2635399.pdf

Mulford, B. (2003b). *The role of school leadership in attracting and retaining teachers and promoting innovative schools and students.* Commissioned paper by the Commonwealth Department of Education Science and Training for their "Review of Teaching and Teacher Education". Retrieved from http://www.dest.gov.au/NR/rdonlyres/161EEEC9-713A-40CD-9E87-2E5A-CA1E19A3/1661/leadership.pdf

Mullen, C. A. (2000). Post-sharkdom: An alternative form of mentoring for teacher educators. In C. A. Mullen, M. D. Cox, C. K. Boettcher, & D. S. Adoue (Eds.), *Breaking the circle of one: Redefining mentorship in the lives and writings of educators* (2nd ed., pp. 145–174). New York, NY: Peter Lang.

Mullen, C. A. (2009). Re-imagining the human dimension of mentoring: A Framework for research administration and the academy. *Journal of Research Administration, 40*(1), 10-22.

Mullen, C. A., Young, J. K., & Harris, S. (2014). Cultural dialogue as social justice advocacy within and beyond university classrooms. In I. Bogotch & C. Shields (Eds.), *International handbook of educational leadership and social [in]justice* (Vol. 2, pp. 1145–1168). Dordrecht, NL: Springer.

Murakami-Ramalho, E., & Panakake, A. (Eds.). (2012). *Educational leaders encouraging the intellectual and professional capacity of others: A social justice agenda*. Charlotte, NC: Information Age Publishing.

Murphy, J., & Vriesenga, M. (2004). *Research on preparation program in educational administration: An analysis*. UCEA Monograph Series. Columbia, MO: University Council for Educational Administration.

Navaratnam, S. (2011). *Guilt, shame and model minorities. How South Asian youth in Toronto navigate the Canadian educational systems*. Unpublished Master's thesis, Department of Sociology and Equity Studies in Education, OISE/University of Toronto.

Nicoletti, C., & Rabe, B. (2012). Productivity of school expenditure: Differences across pupils from diverse backgrounds. *Technical Report*. Institute for Social and Economic Research.

Nieto, S. (2002). *Language, culture, and teaching: Critical perspectives for a new century*. Mahwah, NJ: Lawrence Erlbaum Associates.

Nieto, S. (2004). *Affirming diversity: The sociopolitical context of multicultural education* (4th ed.). New York, NY: Allyn & Bacon.

Noguera, P. (2008). *The trouble with Black boys... And other reflections on race, equity, and the future of public education*. San Francisco, CA: Jossey-Bass.

Normore, A. H. (2008). *Leadership for social justice: Promoting equity and excellence through inquiry and reflective practice*. Charlotte, NC: Information Age Publishing.

Obidah, J. E. (2008). How best to develop preservice teachers' racial and cultural competencies: Reflections on pedagogy and practice in the university classroom. In K. N. Teel & J. E. Obidah (Eds.), *Building racial and cultural competence in he classroom: Strategies from urban educators* (pp. 55–68). New York, NY: Teachers College Press.

OECD. (2001). School factors related to quality and equity. Paris OECD PISA 2012 results, Volume 11. Retrieved from http://www.oecd.org/pisa/keyfindings/pisa-2012-results-volume-ii.htm

Ogbu, J. U. (1991). Low performances as an adaptation: The case of Blacks in Stockton, CA. In M. A. Gibson & J. U. Ogbu (Eds.), *Minority status and schooling* (pp. 249–285). Mahwah, NJ: Lawrence Erlbaum Associates.

Ogbu, J. U. (2003). *Black American students in an affluent suburb: A study of academic disengagement*. Mahwah, NJ: Lawrence Erlbaum Associates.

Ontario Human Rights Commission. (2007). Safe schools settlement reached with the Ministry of Education. Retrieved from http://www.ohrc.on.ca/en/resources/news/backgroundedsettlement

Ontario Ministry of Education. (2010). Ontario leadership strategy: Strong and sustainable leadership for improved student achievement. Retrieved from http://www.edu.gov.on.ca/eng/policyfunding/leadership/OLSPaper_September2010.pdf

Ontario Ministry of Education. (2014). Ontario equity and inclusive strategy. Reach every student: Energizing Ontario education. Retrieved from http://www.edu.gov.on.ca/eng/policyfunding/inclusiveguide.pdf

Ontario Trillium Foundation. (2009, 2010). Diversity in Ontario: A community profile. Retrieved from http://Trilliumfoundations.org/DiversityReportOntarioENGLISH.pdf

Panakake, A., & Abrego, J. (2012). Building capacity: The foundation of developing others. In E. Murakami-Ramhalho & A. Panakake (Eds.), *Educational leaders encouraging the intellectual and professional capacity of others: A social justice agenda* (pp. 3–24). Charlotte, NC: Information Age Publishing.

Paris, D. (2012). Culturally sustaining pedagogy: A needed change in stance, terminology and practice. *Educational Researcher, 41*(3), 93–97.

Paris, D., & Alim, S. (2014). What are we trying to sustain through culturally sustaining pedagogy? A loving critique forward. *Harvard Educational Review, 84*(1), 85–100.

Pinar, W. F. (2007). *Intellectual advancement through disciplinary: Verticality and horizontality in curriculum studies.* Rotterdam, The Netherlands: Sense.

Plummer, K. (2001). *Documents of life: An invitation to a critical humanism.* London: Sage.

Pollock, M. (Ed.). (2008). *Everyday antiracism: Getting real about race in school.* New York, NY: New Press.

Portelli, J. P. (2011). Preface. In R. P. Solomon, J. Singer, A. Campbell, & A. Allen (Eds.), *Brave new teachers: Doing social justice work in neo-liberal times* (pp. vii–xii). Toronto, ON: Canadian Scholars' Press Inc.

Quaye, S. J., & Harper, S. R. (2007). Faculty accountability for culturally-inclusive pedagogy and curricula. *Liberal Education, 93*(3), 32–39.

Quiocho, A., & Rios, F. (2000). The power of their presence: Minority group teachers and schooling. *Review of Educational Research, 70*(4), 485–528.

Reagle, C. (2006). Creating effective schools where all students can learn. *The Rural Education, 27*(3), 24–33.

Reeve, J. (2012). A self determination theory perspective on student engagement. In A. Christenson, A. Reschly, & C. Wylie (Eds.), *Handbook of research on student engagement* (pp. 149–172). New York, NY: Springer.

Reeve, J. M., & Tseng, C. (2011). Agency as a fourth aspect of students' engagement during learning activities. *Contemporary Educational Psychology, 36*(4), 257–267.

Reschly, A. L., & Christenson, S. L. (2012). Jingle, jangle and conceptual haziness: Evolution and future directions of the engagement construct. In A. Christenson, A. Reschly, & C. Wylie (Eds.), *Handbook of research on student engagement* (pp. 3–19). New York, NY: Springer.

Riehl, C. J. (2000). The principal's role in creating inclusive schools for diverse students: A review of normative, empirical, and critical literature on the practice of educational administration. *Review of Educational Research, 70*(1), 55–81. doi:10.3102/00346543070001055.

Roberts, R. (2002). *A passion for good: An autobiography.* Reno, NV: University of Nevada Press.

Ruck, M., & Wortley, S. (2002). Racial and ethnic minority high school students' perceptions of schools disciplinary practices: A look at some Canadian findings. *Journal of Youth and Adolescence, 31*(3), 185–195.

Russo, A. (1991). We cannot live without our lives. In C. Mohanty, A. Russo, & T. Lourdes (Eds.), *Third world women and the politics of feminism* (pp. 297–313). Bloomington: Indiana University Press.

Ryan, J. (2006). *Inclusive leadership.* Indianapolis, IN: Jossey-Bass.

Ryan, J. (2012). *Struggling for inclusion: Educational leadership in a neoliberal world.* Greenwich, CT: Information Age Publishing.

Ryan, J. (2014). Promoting inclusive leadership in diverse schools. In I. Bogotch & C. Shields (Eds.), *International handbook of educational leadership and social (in)justice* (pp. 465–484). Dordrecht, NL: Springer

Ryan, J. (2015). Strategic activism, educational leadership and social justice. *International Journal of Leadership in Education.* 19(1), 87-100 doi:10.1080/13603124.2015.1096077

Ryan, J., Pollock, K., & Antonelli, F. (2007). *Teacher and administrator diversity in Canada: Leaky pipelines, bottlenecks and glass ceilings.* Paper presented at the Canadian Society for Studies in Education (CSSE), Saskatoon, May. Retrieved from http://home.oise.utoronto.ca/~jryan/pub_files/Art.April09.numbers.pdf

Santamarina, C., & Marinas, J. M. (2001). Historias de vida y historia oral. In J. M. Delgado & J. Gutierres (Eds.), *Metodos y tecnieasaualitati vasde investigacion en ciecias sociales* (pp. 259–283). Madrid: Sintesis.

Santoro, N. (2009). Teaching in culturally diverse contexts: What knowledge about 'self' and 'others' do teachers need? *Journal of Education for Teaching, 35*(2), 33–45.

Schlossberg, N. K. (1989). Marginality and mattering: Key issues in building community. *New Directions for Student Services, 48*, 5–15.

Schwalm, H. (2014). *Autobiography. In the living handbook of narratology.* Retrieved from http://www.lhn.uni-hamburg.de/article/autobiography

Schwartz, K. (2014). *Facing race issues in the classroom: How to connect with students.* Retrieved from http://ww2.kqed.org/mindshift/2014/04/04/how-can-teachers-address-race-issues-in-class-ask-students/

Sergiovanni, T. (1992). *Moral leadership.* San Francisco, CA: Jossey-Bass.

Shadiow, L. (1996). Remembering a mentor. *Clearinghouse, 69*(5), 277–279.

Shapiro, J., & Stekovich, J. (2005). *Ethical leadership and decision making in education* (2nd ed.). Mahwah, NJ: Lawrence Erlbaum.

Shapiro, S., & Shapiro, S. (1995). Silent voices, bodies of knowledge: Towards a critical pedagogy of the body. *Journal of Curriculum Theory, 11*(1), 49–72.

Shields, C. M. (2010). Transformative leadership: Working for equity in diverse contexts. *Educational Administration Quarterly, 46*(4), 558–589.

Shields, C. M. (2014). Leadership for social justice: A critical transformative approach. In I. Bogotch & C. Shields (Eds.), *International handbook of educational leadership and social (in)justice* (pp. 323–340). Dordrecht, NL: Springer.

Shields, C. M., & Mohan, E. (2008). High quality education for all students: Putting social justice at its heart. *Teacher Development, 12*(4), 289–300.

Sinatra, G. M., Heddy, B. C., & Lombardi, D. (2015). The challenge of defining and measuring student engagement in science. *Educational Psychologist, 50*(1), 1–13.

Singer, A., & Pezone, M. (2003). Education for social change: From theory to practice. *Workplace: A Journal for Academic Labor, 5*(2), 1-4

Singer, J. (2011). Preparing the equity teacher. In R. P. Solomon, J. Singer, A. Campbell, & A. Allen (Eds.), *Brave new teachers: Doing social justice work in neo-liberal times* (pp. 31–69). Toronto, ON: Canadian Scholars' Press Inc..

Singleton, G. E., & Linton, C. (2006). *Courageous conversations about race: A field guide for achieving equity in schools.* Thousand Oaks, CA: Corwin Press.

Sirotnik, K. A., & Oakes, J. (1986). Critical inquiry for renewal: Liberating theory and practice. In K. A. Sirotnik & J. Oakes (Eds.), *Critical perspectives on the organization and improvement of schooling* (pp. 3–93). Boston, MA: Kluwer Nijhoff.

Sleeter, C. E. (2012). Confronting the marginalization of culturally responsive pedagogy. *Urban Education, 47*(3), 562–584. doi:10.1177/0042085911431472.

Sloterdijk, P. (1978). *Literatur und Organisation von Lebenserfahrung. Autobiographien der Zwanziger Jahre.* München: Hanser.

Smyth, J. (1989). A pedagogical and educative view of leadership. In J. Smyth (Ed.), *Critical perspectives on educational leadership* (pp. 179–204). London: Routledge Falmer.

Solomon, P. R. (1995). Beyond prescriptive pedagogy: Teacher inservice education for cultural diversity. *Journal of Teacher Education, 46*(4), 251–258.

Solomon, P. R. (1997). Race, role-modeling and representation in teacher education and teaching. *Canadian Journal of Education, 22*(4), 395–410.

Solomon, P. R. (2002). School leaders and antiracism: Overcoming pedagogical and political obstacles. *Journal of School Leadership, 12*(2), 174–197.

Solomon, P. R., & Levine-Rasky, C. (1994). *Accommodation and resistance: Educators' responses to multicultural education.* Report to the Canadian Heritage. North York, ON: York University.

Solomon, P. R., & Levine-Rasky, C. (2003). *Teaching for equity and diversity: Research in practice.* Toronto, ON: Canadian Scholars' Press Inc..

Solomon, P. R., Singer, J., Campbell, A., Allen, A., & Portelli, J. P. (2012). *Brave new teachers: Doing social justice work in neo-liberal times.* Toronto, ON: Canadian Scholars' Press Inc..

Solórzano, D. G., & Villalpando, O. (1998). Critical race theory, marginality, and the experience of minority students in higher education. In C. Torres & T. Mitchell (Eds.), *Emerging issues in the sociology of education: Comparative perspectives* (pp. 211–224). New York, NY: State University of New York Press.

Solorzano, D. G., & Yosso, T. J. (2001). Critical race methodology: Counter story-telling as an analytical framework for education research. *Qualitative Inquiry, 8*(1), 23–44.

Sparks, D. (2005). *Leading for results: Transforming, learning, and relationships in schools.* Thousand Oaks, CA: Corwin Press.

Spring, J. (2001). *Globalization and educational rights: An intercivilizational analysis.* Mahwah, NJ: Lawrence Erlbaum Associates.

Statistics Canada. (2011). *Canada yearbook.* Retrieved from http://www.statscan.bc.ca/pub/11-402-X/2011000/chap/imm/imm-eng.htm

Steele, C. M. (1997). A threat in the air: How stereotypes shape intellectual identity and performance. *American Psychologist, 52*(6), 613–629.

Sue, S., & Okazaki, S. (1990). Asian American education achievements. A phenomenon in search of an explanation. *American Psychologist, 45*(8), 913–920.

Sughrue, J. (2003). Zero tolerance for children: Two wrongs do not make a right. *Educational Administration Quarterly, 39*(2), 238–258.

Tamar, G. (2013). Imagination: *The Stanford Encyclopedia of Philosophy.* Retrieved from http://plato.stanford.edu/archives/fall2013/entries/imagination/

Tatum, B. D. (2001). Defining racism: Can we talk? In P. Rothenberg (Ed.), *Race, class, and gender in the United States: An integrated study* (pp. 100–107). New York, NY: Worth.

Taylor, L., & Parsons, J. (2011). Improving student engagement. *Current Issues in Education, 14*(1). Retrieved from http://cle.asu.edu/

Teelucksingh, C. C. (2006). Toward claiming space in Canadian cities. In C. Teeluchsingh (Ed.), *Claiming space: Racialization in Canadian cities* (pp. 1–17). Waterloo, ON: Wilfred Laurier University Press.

The Institute for Educational Leadership. (2013). *The Ontario leadership framework: A school and system leader's guide to putting Ontario's leadership framework into action.* Retrieved from https://iel.immix.ca/storage/6/1380680840/OLF_User_Guide_FINAL.pdf

Theoharis, G. (2007). Social justice educational leaders and resistance: Toward a theory of social justice leadership. *Educational Administration Quarterly, 43*(2), 221–258.

Thompson, P. (2001). How principals lose 'face': A disciplinary tale of educational administration and modern managerialism. *Disocurse: Studies in the Cultural Politics of Education, 22*(1), 5–22. doi:10.1080/01596300120039722.

Tierney, W. G., & Sallee, M. W. (2008). *"Praxis." The Sage encyclopedia of qualitative research methods.* Thousand oaks, CA: Sage Publications.

Toure, J. L. (2008). *"There's some good karma up in here". A case study of white school leadership in an urban context.* Doctoral dissertation. Available from ProQuest dissertations and theses database (UMI No. 3349246).

Turhan, M. (2010). Social justice leadership: Implications for roles and responsibilities of school administrators. *Procedia—Social and Behavioral Sciences, 9*, 1357–1361.

Turner, T. (2015). *Voices of Black educators: An experiential report.* Retrieved from http://onabse.org/ONABSE_VOICES_OF_BLACK_EDUCATORS_Final_Report.pdf

Tyack, D. (1974). *The one best system.* Cambridge, MA: Harvard University Press.

Tyack, D., & Cuban, L. (1995). *Tinkering toward utopia: A century of public school reform.* Cambridge, MA: Harvard University Press.

United States Department of Commerce. (2015). Retrieved from http://www/census.gov/content/dam/Census/library/publications/2015/demo/p25-1143.pdf?

US News and World Report. (2015). Retrieved from http://www.usnews.com/news/blog/data-mine/2015/01/28/us-education-still-separate-and-unequal

Utsey, S. O., & Ponterotto, J. G. (1996). Development and validation of the Index of Race-Related Stress (IRRS). *Journal of Counseling Psychology, 43*(4), 490–502.

Vassallo, B. (2015). Towards a framework for culturally responsive educational leadership. *International Journal of Learning, Teaching and Educational Research, 12*(2), 107–120.

Villegas, A. M., & Luca, T. (2004). Diversifying the teacher workforce: A retrospective and prospective analysis. In M. Smylie & D. Miiretkzky (Eds.), *Addressing teacher workforce issues effectively: Institutional, political, and philosophical barriers* (pp. 70–104). Chicago, IL: National Society for the Study of Education.

Villegas, A. M., Strom, K., & Lucas, T. (2012). Closing the racial/ethnic gap between students of color and their teachers: An elusive goal. *Equity & Excellence in Education, 45*(2), 283–301.

Waite, D., Turan, S., & Nino, J. M. (2014). Schools for capitalism, corporativism, and corruption: Examples from Turkey and the USA. In I. Bogotch & C. M. Shields (Eds.), *International handbook of educational leadership and social (in) justice* (pp. 619–642). Dordrecht, NL: Springer.

Walker, A., & Dimmock, C. (2005). Leading the multiethnic school: Research evidence on successful practice. *The Educational Forum, 69*(2), 291–304.

Ware, F. (2006). Warm demander pedagogy culturally responsive teaching that supports a culture of achievement for African American students. *Urban Education, 41*(4), 427–456. doi:10.1177/0042085906289710.

Wasden, D. (1988). *The mentoring handbook.* Provo, UT: Brigham Young University.

Wessler, S. F. (2011). Confronting racial and religious tensions. *Educational Leadership, 69*(1), 36–39.

White, R. C., & Cooper, K. (2012). Critical leadership and social justice: Research, policy and educational practice. *US-China Education Review A, 5*, 517–532. Retrieved from http://files.eric.ed.gov/fulltextED534295.pdf

Willms, J. D., Friesen, S., & Milton, P. (2009). What did you do in school today? Transforming classrooms through social academic and intellectual engagement. *First National Report.* Toronto, ON: Canadian Education Association.

Wilson-Forsberg, S. (2012). *Getting used to the quiet: Immigrant adolescents' journey to belonging in New Brunswick, Canada.* Montreal, QC: McGill-Queen's University Press.

Yeh, C. J. (2001). An exploratory study if school counsellor's experiences with and perceptions of Asian-American students. *Professional School Counselling, 4*(5), 349–356.

Yin, X. H. (2000). The two sides of Americas model minority. *Los Angeles Times*, Part M.

Young, M., & Lopez, G. R. (2005). The nature of inquiry in educational leadership. In F. W. English (Ed.), *The Sage handbook of educational leadership: Advances in theory, research, and practice* (pp. 337–361). Thousand Oaks, CA: Sage.

Zeichner, K. (2009). *Teacher education and the struggle for social justice.* New York, NY: Routledge.

Zey, M. G. (1984). *The mentor connection.* Homewood, IL: Dow Jones-Irwin.

Zúñiga, X., Nagda, B., & Sevig, T. (2002). Intergroup dialogues: An educational model for cultivating engagement across differences. *Equity & Excellence in Education, 6*(1), 115–132.

Zyngier, D. (2008). Re-conceptualising student engagement: Doing education not doing time. *Teaching and Teacher Education, 24*(7), 1765–1776.

Author Index

A.E. Lopez, *Culturally Responsive and Socially Just Leadership in Diverse Contexts*, DOI 10.1057/978-1-137-53339-5

Subject Index

A.E. Lopez, *Culturally Responsive and Socially Just Leadership in Diverse Contexts*, DOI 10.1057/978-1-137-53339-5

D

CPSIA information can be obtained
at www.ICGtesting.com
Printed in the USA
LVHW082156250822
726919LV00004B/93

9 781137 533388